G000273289

Nottingham Forest F.C.

The Official Illustrated History

contents

Welcome to the *Official Illustrated History of Nottingham Forest*. While this isn't the first time that a pictorial history of the club has been prepared we feel that it is the largest, most colourful and most in-depth one ever attempted.

Few Clubs in world football can claim to have a history as rich and exciting as that of Nottingham Forest. From the numerous innovations of the 19th century which included early floodlights, the first shin pads, tactical revolutions and more for over 140 years. Domestic and European heartbreak was more than outweighed by a glorious haul of trophies.

The book you are now holding has been two years in the making and draws on material provided by the club, ex-players and long-time collectors. We make use of programmes, letters, documents, plans, maps, football cards and stickers, newspaper cuttings, cartoons, photographs, sketches, and more. It's all used to showcase the development of Nottingham Forest on and off the field since the 1860s and even earlier.

As well as the chronological history of the Reds, this project highlights such areas as the grounds that Forest have called home, the many trophies won, the different kits and emblems that the club has sported and some of the more unusual stories from almost a century and a half. We have rewards being offered, great escapes being made, wins against the odds and flat out failures.

We eventually gathered so much material that it was a difficult task to narrow down what we could actually use. We twice had to expand the number of pages in this book and we still have enough material left for more volumes in the future. Right up to the printing deadline we were unearthing more material and we are still keen to do so, especially from the families of ex-Forest players from before the Second World War.

The images were chosen on the basis of one of several criteria: rare and previously unseen images, historically important images, famous 'iconic' images. With these criteria in mind it follows that some images will have been used many times before, but if they have we've tried to look for alternatives (for example the 1979 European Cup Final goal). It also follows that some of the oldest material will be of poorer quality than we would have liked, but due to its importance we've still used it when possible.

Many people were involved in putting this all together and we are especially grateful to everyone who allowed us to use items from personal collections, they are all credited individually elsewhere in this volume.

We hope you enjoy looking through these pictures as much as we did researching them and putting it all together,

Pineapple Books, September 2009

Introduction

In The Beginning…
(1865 and all that)

Classical continued.

1060 Thomas Henry Guilford · 11 · 0 Hannah Guilford, Wid. Mansfield Road

1061 George Nicholstone · 10 · 4 Samuel Moore, Solr. Low Pavement

1062 John Reddish · 10 · 2 John Reddish, Police Sr. intend. Fletcher Gate

1063 Marcus Lewis · 9 · 2 Henry Lewis, Slater, Lenside

1064 James Tomlinson · 8 · 10 Jas. Tomlinson Junr. Merch. Castle Terrace

1065 Francis John Burton 8 · 9 Francis Burton, Attorney Clerk, Mansfield Road

English

1066 Wm. Corbian Bearder · 12 · 9 John Bearder, Greenr. Cemetery Road

1067 James Cockayne · 12 · 0 Jas. Cockayne, Milkn. Sidney Street

1068 Samuel Annibal · 12 · 0 Richard Annibal, Rr. Long Row

1069 Samuel Pegg · 12 · 0 William Pegg, Leather Cutter, Hollow Stone

1070 George Storer · 11 · 9 Sophia Storer, Poulterer Fletcher Gate

English Department.

43. George Harrison · 14 · 6 George Harrison, Miller (at Mr. Druggist, Chapel)

44. John Robert Wilson 12 · 6 An Orphan, grandmother's Robinson, at 5 Bilbie Street

45. Henry Abbey — — 12 · 7 Mark Abbey, Mount Vernon

46. Theophilus Bunney 12 · 4 William Bunney, Books. Bridle

47. William Hodgson · 11 · 3 Thomas Hodgson, Overlooker at Gt. Freeman St.

48. John Parr · 11 · 2 Richard Parr, Sheridan St.

49. Walter Cockayne · 10 · 9 William Cockayne, Butcher, Middle

50. Charles Robinson · 10 · 8 Samuel Robinson, Collector, Add.

51. Henry Samuel Smith 10 · 6 James Smith, per, Chapel St.

52. Thos. George Howitt · 10 · 1 Thomas Howitt, Printer, Woodl.

53. Edwin Gordon — 10 · 9 Edwin Herbord

[above] Forest had several links with the Nottingham High School in the early years. Here we have two High School register entries for boys who went on to be founder members of The Forest Foot Ball Club. The left one shows James Tomlinson's entry in 1852 and on the right we have Thomas George Howitt in 1859. Tomlinson didn't exactly get a glowing report from the school which said, "Very slow. Removed at last by his father rather than comply with the rule not to let him be absent without previous leave."

[previous page] The Forest Recreation Ground was the club's first home. This photograph, taken around 20 years after Forest played their last game on the site, shows a cricket match taking place where Forest once played out their Saturday afternoons.

[below] The Forest Grandstand with railings visible for the horse racing.

[above] Richard Daft and an advert for his sports shop in Nottingham. At the original meeting to form a football club it was decided to purchase a set of red caps to wear during games, as was usual at the time. William Brown was thus dispatched to Richard Daft's shop to buy the caps and ensure that Forest would forever have red as their colour.

[below] The Clinton Arms on Shakespeare Street, the site of many early Forest meetings in the 1860s and the venue for after match socialising. The building still stands today with the outside looking almost unchanged.

The Clinton Arms Nottm

THE NOTTINGHAM FOREST FOOTBALL CLUB.

Shrove-Tuesday Afternoon, Half-past Two o'clock, a Game at FOOTBALL will be played, between sides chosen by Mr. C. Daft and Mr. H. Rastil, on the Forest Grounds.

The public are requested to keep outside the Flag boundary lines.   JOHN MILFORD, Hon. Sec.

THE NOTTINGHAM FOREST FOOT-BALL CLUB.

—Weather permitting, Ball kicked off every Saturday Afternoon. at 2.30 on the Forest Cricket ground.

T. MILFORD, Hon. Sec.

FOOTBALL—NOTTS. v. FOREST.—The closing match of the Notts. Club will be played on Thursday next, on the Meadows' ground—13 of the Notts. playing 15 of the Forest. Kick off at three p.m.

FOOTBALL.—NOTTS. v. FOREST CLUB.—The return match was played yesterday, ten of the Forest club competing against eleven of the Notts. club, on the Meadows cricket-ground, and after a pleasant and well-contested game, resulted in a draw, neither sides winning a goal. John Bradley, Esq., officiated as umpire for both clubs. Many splendid kicks were made by both sides, Mr. Baillon, of the Notts. club, particularly excelling. The sides were as under:—Forest club, Messrs. Milford, Barks, Ford, Gamble, Tudor, Herbert, Richardson, Bell, Lymberry, and Cooke. Notts. club, Messrs. Hack, Baillon, Steegmann, Scrimshaw, Elliott, Ward, Wardle, Lees, Wilkinson, Wright, and Stranger.

THE Members of the Forest Foot Ball Club are

requested to meet for practice, on the Forest Cricket Ground, at 2.30 this day, preparatory to a match between Notts. F.B.C. v. F.F.B.C., to be played on Thursday next, on the Meadows Cricket Ground.   JNO. MILFORD, Hon. Sec.

12507

Six newspaper entries from 1866, dated (from top to bottom) as follows: February 13th, 17th, March 22nd, April 19th, 20th and December 8th.

[left] Sam Weller Widdowson was one of the greatest football innovators of the Victorian age. He patented the first shin pads and was instrumental in the introduction of the 2-3-5 formation and the use of the referee's whistle. He was an all-round athlete (an accomplished sprinter and hurdler) as well as serving Forest as a player from 1869 to 1891. He is still the Reds' all-time leading FA Cup goal scorer with 19 goals scored in only 23 games.

[following page] W.H. Revis was, at the age of just 16, a founder member of Forest in 1865. He scored several goals during the first years that the Reds played organised games.

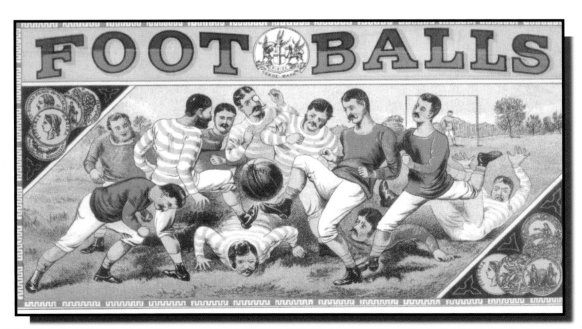

[above] A collection of Forest's greatest athletes. Left to right: Sam Widdowson, Charles Daft, C J Spencer, C Gowthorpe, S Bestow.

[left] A Forest Sports medal won by the great Tinsley Lindley and an advert for the first athletics day which would become the Forest Sports for many years to come. As well as a number of athletics events the day included a velocipede race (cycling) and a competition to see who could kick a football the furthest. Crowds at these athletics days soon grew to almost 20,000 while the football was getting around a tenth of that number.

Nottingham Forest Football Club

Athletic Sports.

March 3rd 1871

My Lord

On behalf of the
committee of the Forest Football
Club we beg to thank you
for permitting us the honor
of placing your name upon
our patrons list this year.

We beg also to remind
your lordship that last year

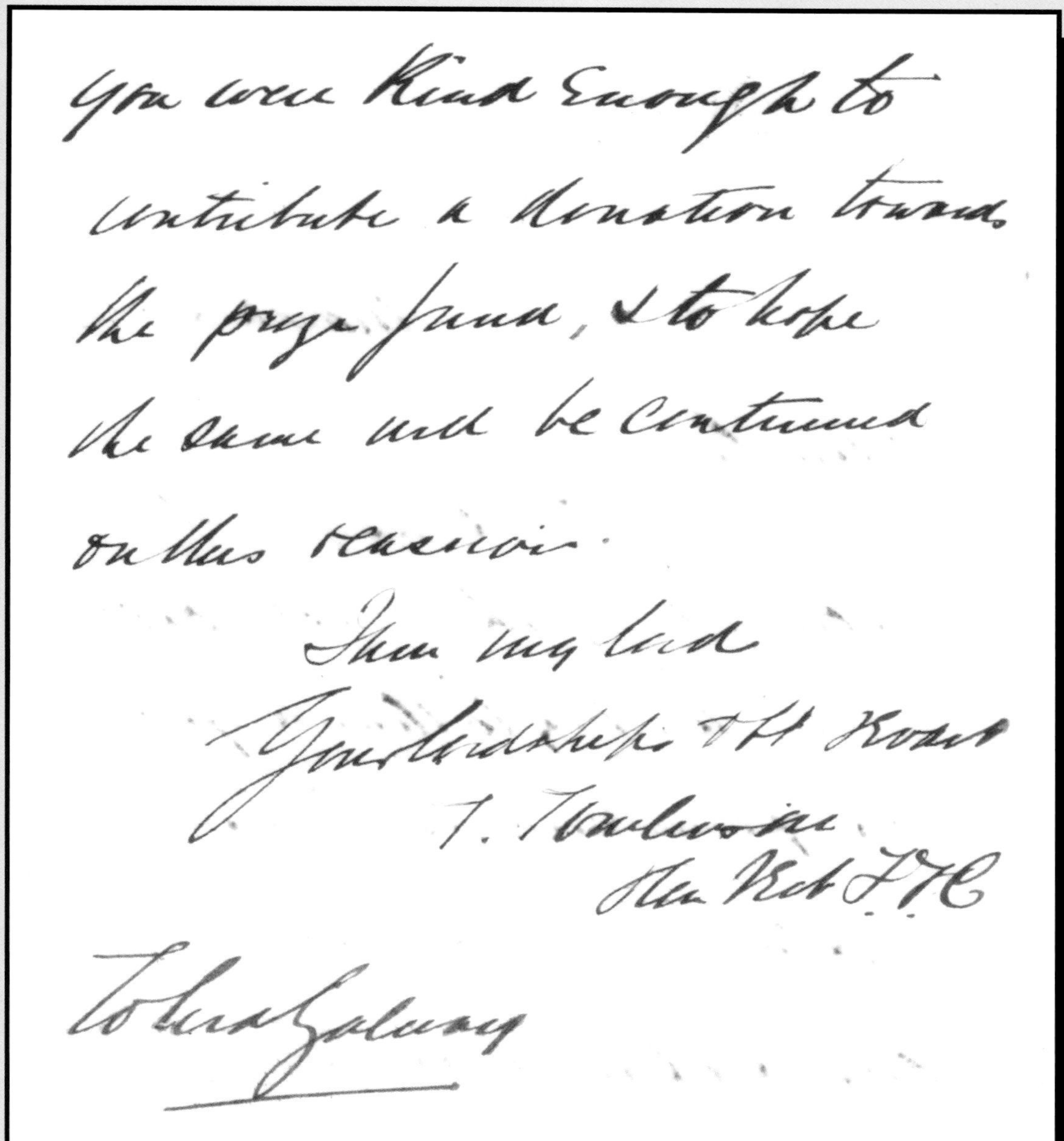

You were kind enough to contribute a donation towards the prize fund, & to hope the same will be continued on this occasion.

Then my lord

Your lordships &c

T. Townsend

Hon Sec F.F.C

To Lord Galway

This letter highlights the earliest known piece of club stationery. The club was writing to Lord and Lady Galway thanking them for helping the last athletics sports day and fishing for more funds for the following year. It reads: "My Lord, on behalf of the committee of the Forest Football Club we beg to thank you for permitting us the honour of placing your name upon the patrons list this year. We beg also to remind your lordships that last year you were kind enough to contribute a donation towards the prize fund and to hope the same will be continued on this occasion."

Boys of the Old Brigade

Notts. County in their very early days, when whiskers were more impressive than trousers.
Names (not in order):

Everall, Sam Widdowson, Revis, W. N. Robinson, F. Marriott, J. Parr, J. Bright, A. Bright, T. C. Spencer, A. W. Cursham, Harwood, Greenhalgh.

"The Boys of the Old Brigade" was run in a 1949 edition of the Nottingham Guardian and showed an early Notts County team photo featuring several Forest players. Widdowson, Revis and Spencer all represented the Reds.

FOOTBALL.

NOTTINGHAM FOREST v. NOTTS. CLUB.

ASSOCIATION CUP TIE.

One of the most interesting matches of the football season in Notts. was that played on the Beeston Cricket Ground, on Saturday last, between the Forest and Notts. Clubs, who had both entered into competition for the Association Challenge Cup, and were drawn together in the first round of ties. The match was played at Beeston, in consequence of the Trent Bridge Ground being engaged for the purpose of a handicap, and the ground was partially enclosed, in order that gate-money might be charged, in order that gate-money might be charged. The trains leaving Nottingham about two o'clock were crowded with people, and there would be probably five hundred persons on the ground, notwithstanding the inclemency of the weather, whilst many took their stand upon the platform of the station, whence a good view of the game was obtained. Both teams were well represented, and a spirit of emulation as to which club was best worthy of representing the town in the football field contributed to make the game of a much more exciting character than usual. Owing to the recent rains the ground was in a very sodden condition, and as a matter of course the going was very heavy, whilst half a breeze blew from the station end of the ground towards the pavilion.

FOOTBALL.

OLD ETONIANS v. NOTTINGHAM FOREST.—Despite a bitterly cold wind there was a very fair attendance of spectators at Kennington Oval, on Saturday afternoon, to witness the single game in the fifth ties of the Association Challenge Cup. The contending clubs were the old Etonians and Nottingham Forest—the two teams which from the commencement of the competition have shown the most consistent and excellent form. It was a terribly unpleasant and trying afternoon for onlookers, but those who were present had an ample reward. Certainly so fast and well-contested a game has not been seen, under Association rules this season, the spectators were not slow to recognise the excellence of the play, and from start to finish the greatest excitement prevailed. Notts. Forest lost the services of Mr. Earp, for whom, however, an efficient substitute was found in Mr. Bishop. The elevens were as follows:—*Old Etonians :* Hon. A. F. Kinnaird (captain), E. Christian and Edgar Lubbock (half-backs), L. Bury and H. H. Calvert, (backs), H Whitfield, H. C. Goodhart, H. B. Sedgwick, R. D. Anderson, C. J. Clerke and J. Hawtrey, (goal). *Notts. Forest :*—S. W. Widdowson (captain), C. J. Caborn (back), E. Luntley and W. Luntley (three-quarter backs), A. J. Bates and M. Holrood (half-backs), J. P. Turner, A. H. Smith, J. Bishop, A. C. Goodyer, and J. Sands (goal). Messrs. Hubert Heron and E. D. Ellis were umpires, and Mr. C. W. Alcock acted as referee. Notts. Forest won the toss and chose to have the strong wind in their favour for the first half of the game. It was soon seen that the play would be of more than ordinary interest. Both sides from the first did their very best, and certainly nothing was lost for want of trying. Having the wind to help them the Nottingham men of course played an offensive game, charging down upon their opponents time after time in brilliant style. The Eton backs and half-backs were kept fully employed, and in defending his goal Christian certainly showed the finest play of the afternoon. The kicking of the Nottingham men was not so accurate as in some matches, but probably the wind was in a great measure answerable for this. Many shots at goal went very wide. Do all they would the Notts. men could not gain any material advantage, and so "half-time arrived without a goal having been obtained on either side. The change of ends was received with great applause by the supporters of the Etonians, and on the ball being re-started the interest in the game became greater than ever. For a few minutes the ball was kept in the Eton half of the ground, but before long it was taken right over, and then Whitfield kicked the first goal of the match. This disaster incited the Notts. men to even greater efforts. Despite the wind they carried the ball across to the Etonians' end, and after some very clever passing, Bishop, with a good kick, made the score equal. From this point the game was fast and furious. Four corner kicks fell to the Etonians, and once a similar advantage was gained by Nottingham. Nothing was done, however, and it began to look as though the game would have to be prolonged for an extra half-hour. The Etonians worked desperately, and at last they had their reward. A fine piece of play by Sedgwick put the ball right in front of the Nottingham goal. A short but fierce scrimmage took place, the end of which was that the ball touched one of the Notts. men and went through the goal. In the ten minutes that remained the Notts. men tried hard to retrieve themselves, but to no purpose. The call of time left the Old Etonians winners of a splendid game by two goals to one, and they will now have to play the Clapham Rovers for possession of the cup.

A report of Forest's first ever competitive game, a first round FA Cup game against Notts County on November 16th 1878. Forest won 3-1, then beat Sheffield, Old Harovians and Oxford University before losing to the Old Etonians in the semi-final.

The earliest known Forest team picture. Standing at back; Charles Caborn, John Sands, Edwin Luntley. Middle row; A. J. Bates, A. W. Smith, A. M. Holroyd, J. P. Turner, Walter Luntley. Front row; Arthur Goodyer, Sam Widdowson, F. W. Earp. Several versions of this picture exist, indeed the one shown here has been doctored to show the England emblem on four internationals.

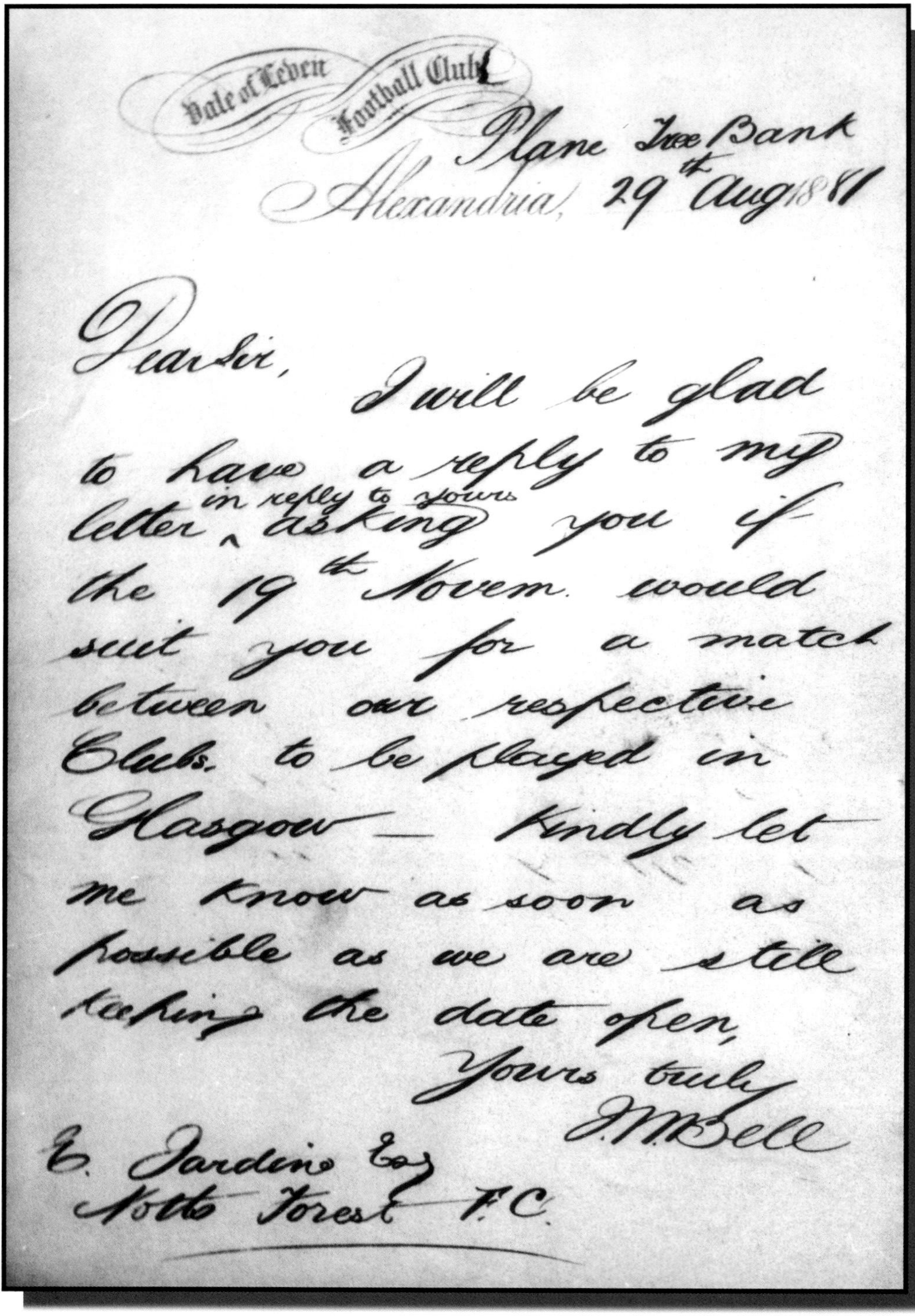

Vale of Leven Football Club

Plane Tree Bank
Alexandria, 29th Aug 1881

Dear Sir,

I will be glad to have a reply to my letter in reply to yours asking you if the 19th Novem. would suit you for a match between our respective Clubs. to be played in Glasgow — Kindly let me know as soon as possible as we are still keeping the date open,

Yours truly
J. McBell

C. Jardine Esq
Notts Forest F.C.

Vale of Leven write to Forest asking for a game
in the 1881-82 season, but it was never arranged.

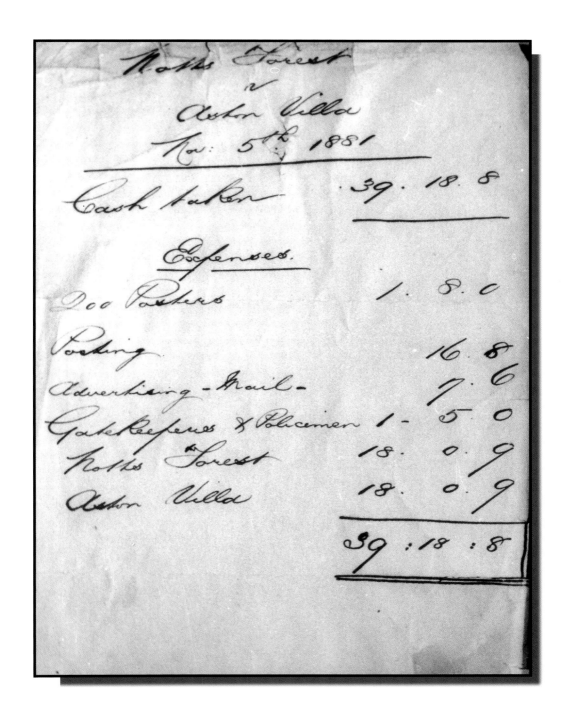

Notts Forest
v
Aston Villa
Nov: 5th 1881

Cash taken   39 . 18 . 8

Expenses.

200 Posters   1 . 8 . 0

Posting   16 . 8

Advertising — Mail —   7 . 6

Gatekeepers & Policemen   1 — 5 . 0

Notts Forest   18 . 0 . 9

Aston Villa   18 . 0 . 9

     39 : 18 : 8

Accounts for the 1881 first round FA Cup tie at Aston Villa which Forest lost 4-1. The Forest share would be worth about £870 today!

THE DARWEN FOOTBALL CLUB.

WINNERS OF THE

LANCASHIRE FOOTBALL

ASSOCIATION CHALLENGE CUP

DARWEN

Dec 8th 1881

Dear Sir,

Seeing that you been disappointed & so shabbily treated by Lancashire clubs lately it is with extreme regret that I have to ask you to postpone our match with you at Nottingham on Saturday Dec 17th. It is the only date we can arrange our English Cup tie with Turton except one & that date we have Queen's Park there. I have not yet had a committee meeting but I have written this as soon as arrangements are completed. Have done all I can to avoid this but could not. I will write you further as to date on which we shall be able to come

Yours truly
B Harwood

E Gardine Esq
Notts

Darwen had to cancel this planned game because
of a forthcoming cup tie.

55 John Brown St

ESTABLISHED 1874.

WANDERERS' FOOTBALL CLUB,

Bolton, Feb 12th 1881

Dear Sir
    Your note to hand. —
I see from your remarks that
You cannot play us a return
match &you also ask me to
send our open dates. — If
you will refer back to my last
letter you will see that I sent
one of our match cards. So that
you could select any date we
have open from it. — I think a
mistake must have been made, as
the writer of your letter asks me to
send our open dates, when I have
already sent same, he also addresses
me as, Hon Sec. Blackburn Rovers. —
Kindly say which date you select
    Truly yours
    J Rawsthorn.

Confusion arose with Wanderers in this letter about
who was supposed to play who, where and when.

207. Derby Road. Lenton. Nott⁵. J.Spree.

Forest moved to Lenton in 1882 to play at the Parkside Ground just off Derby Road. The pitch was sloping and the facilities generally lacking. Three years later they moved down the hill to the Gregory Ground on the other side of Lenton Boulevard. The postcard above shows a tram by the side of where the ground would have been. Forest could sometimes get crowds of 2,000 to 3,000 at this venue and trams would ferry fans from the site of the present day Broadmarsh Centre to the ground every few minutes. Below is a photo of the site today with the last remaining grassed area which is significantly smaller than at the time that Forest played there.

An architect's sketch of a stand proposed for the Gregory Ground.

Football.

WEDNESBURY CHARITY CUP.—The final tie for this cup was played on Saturday, when the Forest Club won by five goals to three.

When Forest won their first ever trophy, beating West Bromwich Albion in the Wednesbury Cup in 1883, the local press were less than overcome with excitement. This was the whole report of the game.

When Forest lost an FA Cup replay at Sheffield Wednesday Sam Widdowson was so sure that the Yorkshire side had fielded ineligible players that he personally put up posters around Sheffield offering a reward for information.

SHEFFIELD WEDNESDAY v. NOTTING-HAM FOREST.

£20 REWARD.

Considerable sensation was caused in Sheffield and district yesterday by the appearance of bills on the walls announcing that Mr. S. W. Widdowson, of Nottingham, would give a reward of £20 to any person who can prove that W. Harrison, of Redcar, W. Betts, of Pyebank, and J. Bentley, of Walkley, were not members of the Sheffield Wednesday Football Club before Dec. 6th last. The reward bears upon the recent tie for the English Cup between Sheffield Wednesday and Nottingham Forest, in which the latter were defeated by three goals to two. The Forest allege that the three men named were not *bona fide* members of the Wednesday Club, and that consequently they ought to be disqualified. The matter is under consideration by the Executive of the English Association, and what course they will adopt is being strongly debated.

BOROUGH OF NOTTINGHAM.

BYE-LAWS, 1870, AS TO NEW STREETS & BUILDINGS

(21 AND 22 VICT.,   CAP. 98, SEC. 34.)

[AS TO NEW BUILDINGS.]

Fourteen Days' Notice by the   to the Borough Surveyor,

as to intention to erect New Buildings.

TO THE SURVEYOR OF THE CORPORATION OF NOTTINGHAM.

SIR,

WE do hereby give you Notice, That WE intend to* *Erect a Wooden Pavilion on the Gregory (or Forest Football) Ground Derby Road Lenton*

and herewith WE have deposited at your Office, (St. Peter's Church Side) Detail Plans, Sections, and Block Plan of the intended "New Buildings," drawn to the Scales and shewing the several particulars required in the 20th Clause of the above Bye-Laws, and also have supplied a description of the Materials proposed to be used, and of the intended mode of Drainage and Water Supply.

And that *Ourselves* of *Lenton*

are is to be the *Builders* to have charge of the Buildings so intended

to be erected.

DATED this *5th* day of *January* 188*8*

Signature, *Marshall Bros W.H.*

Address, *Lenton*

---

* Here insert a description of the intended "New Buildings" in general terms, and state how far they relate to any of the following matters :—"The Erection of any New Buildings," or "the making of any Addition to or Alteration in any Building," or "the doing of any matter or thing by the above Bye-Laws placed under the superintendence of the Borough Surveyor."

NOTE.—The attention of every Person intending to lay out New Streets or to erect New Buildings, is particularly called to the whole of the Bye-Laws in respect thereof, as their several enactments will be rigidly enforced.

Planning application for a new stand at the Gregory Ground, 1888.

Football Match—FOREST v. GREAT LEVER,

Trent Bridge Ground, Nottingham, Feb. 17, 1885.

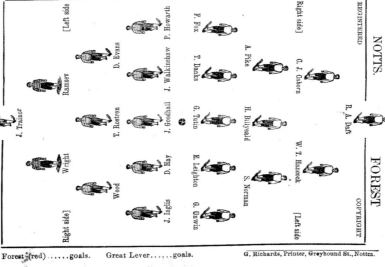

NOTTS.

REGISTERED

FOREST

COPYRIGHT

[Right side] [Left side]

O. J. Caborn

F. Fox

A. Pike

T. Danks

H. Billyeald

S. Norman

R. A. Daft

W. T. Hancock

G. Tutin

E. D. Hay

E. Leighton

G. Unwin

J. Inglis

LEVER

GREAT

[Left side] [Right side]

P. Howarth

D. Evans

W. Watkinson

L. Goodwin

T. Roston

Wright

Wood

Ramsey

J. Tranor

ENGLISH ASSOCIATION CUP.—DRAW FOR SIXTH ROUND.

Old Etonians v. Notts. Forest
Notts. Club v. Queen's Park

West Bromwich Albion v. Blackburn Rovers
Church v. Chatham or Old Carthusians

In order to leave but eight clubs in, seven of the nine received byes in the fifth round, whilst the other couple, Chatham and Old Carthusians met on Feb. 7th, the latter winning by 3 to 0.

Forest (red) ......goals.   Great Lever ......goals.

G. Richards, Printer, Greyhound St., Nottm.

Tinsley Lindley, shown here in his cricket attire, was one of Forest's greatest 19th Century players. While still a student at the High School he signed up for the Forest reserves in 1881 and scored 85 goals in his first season! The following year he was promoted to the first team and notched four on his debut, a 6-1 win over Wolverhampton on February 17th 1883. Lindley then went to study at Cambridge University but played for both teams during the next few years. An all-rounder, he also played cricket and rugby for the university, he graduated as a lawyer and was given an O.B.E. in 1918. By then he had served as Forest's captain and played for the Reds until 1892

Martin Earp served Forest for many years after his playing days were over in 1884.

[above left] Glasgow Rangers played a high profile friendly in Nottingham under prototype floodlights.

Advert for the first Forest Season tickets.

RULES

OF THE

NOTTINGHAM FOREST

Football Club.

ESTABLISHED 1865.

NOTTINGHAM:
T. PICKERILL AND SONS, PRINTERS, HOUNDS GATE.

1887.

OFFICERS.

President.

COLONEL SEELY, J.P.

Vice-Presidents.

A. MORLEY, Esq., M.P.

H. S. WRIGHT, Esq., M.P.

J. A. JACOBY, Esq., M.P.

L. LINDLEY, Esq., J.P.

J. TURNER, Esq., J.P., (Mayor.)

J. BURTON, Esq., J.P.

CAPT. W. E. DENISON.

H. HEYMANN, Esq.

S. W. WIDDOWSON, Esq.

T. G. HOWITT, Esq.

Committee.

Mr. A. J. BATES,

Mr. J. E. BRYAN,

Mr. C. J. CABORN,

Mr. W. HOWELL,

Mr. L. O. LINDLEY.

Mr. E. LUNTLEY,

Mr. T. RADFORD,

Mr. G. SELDON,

Mr. J. SANDS,

Mr. A. W. WARD.

Hon. Secretary.

Mr. C. A. RASTALL.

Financial Secretary.

Mr. W. BROWN.

Hon. Treasurer.

Mr. S. W. WIDDOWSON.

RULES.

1.—That the Club be called "THE NOTTINGHAM FOREST FOOTBALL CLUB."

2.—That the officers of the Club consist of a President, Ten Vice-Presidents, a Secretary, a Treasurer, and Ten Committeemen, all of whom shall be elected by ballot at each Annual General Meeting, and in whom shall be vested the management of the Club, each of them having an equal vote. Six of the said officers shall form a quorum.

3.—That any gentleman wishing to join the Club, shall be proposed by a Member of the Club to the Secretary, who shall nominate him at the next Meeting of the Committee; and that an interval of at least seven days shall take place between such nomination and election.

4.—That the annual subscription of all new Members shall be Ten Shillings; that the annual subscription of all old playing Members shall be Seven Shillings and Sixpence; and that the annual subscription of all old non-playing Members shall be Five Shillings. The whole of the above subscriptions are due in advance on the First of October in each year. The subscription of Honorary Members shall be One Guinea.

5.—That any Member failing to pay his Annual Subscription before the First of January, shall have notice of such non-payment sent him by post, and if such subscription be not paid before the First of February, he shall cease to be a Member of the Club, and his name shall be erased from the books accordingly, unless some explanation satisfactory to the Committee be given ; nevertheless his liability for the current subscription shall continue ; and any Member not having discharged all other liabilities which he may have incurred to the Club before the First of April shall not be allowed to take part in the ensuing Athletic Sports.

6.—That the Annual General Meeting shall be held on the Wednesday of the

last week in August of each year, or earlier, at the discretion of the Committe.

7.— That the team to represent the Club in each match shall be chosen by the Committee, who shall also elect a Captain for the match ; and that all the Members of the team shall act strictly according to the directions of the Captain.

8.—That a special General Meeting of the Members may be called at any time by, and in the name of, the Committee, and shall be summoned by the Secretary, on a requisition in writing signed by ten Members of the Club. That the subject intended to be submitted shall be stated in the notice convening the meeting ; and the discussion and business shall be strictly confined thereto,

and such subject shall not again be discussed at any subsequent Meeting, within a period of six months.

9.—That no resolution shall be passed at any General Meeting unless at least twenty Members are present when the vote is taken.

10.—That in case the misconduct of any Member by impropriety of language or otherwise shall appear to a majority of Members present at a General Meeting, to justify expulsion, he shall thereupon cease to be a Member of the Club.

11.—That no alteration shall be made in these Rules, except at an Annual General Meeting of Members, or at a General Meeting specially convened for the purpose, in conformity with Rule 8,

and notice of any proposed alteration shall be given in writing to the Secretary, at least Fourteen days prior to the Meeting, and shall be notified to all the Members of the Club in convening the Meeting.

12.—That a Special General Meeting shall be called for the second Wednesday in January of each year to elect a Committee of Fourteen Members of the Club, with power to add to their number, for the sole management of the Annual Athletic Sports, and such Committee shall elect from their own number, a Secretary and Treasurer.

13.—That the Accident Fund established November 15th. 1871, shall be sustained, and shall be managed as provided in the following Rules.

[top] When they refused to embrace professionalism, Forest became founder members of the Football Alliance in 1889. The Reds improved each season and in the 1892 pipped Newton Heath (the future Manchester United) by two points to win the championship.

[middle] The Reds then moved to the Football League where they met Bolton Wanderers.

[bottom] The Reds' new ground was the Town Ground near to Trent Bridge just off Arkwright Street.

[opposite page] Arthur Pike played for Forest from 1888 until 1895 scoring 27 goals in 110 League and Cup games. Here he poses in the playing kit of the day.

[previous pages, 32-33] This previously unpublished photograph seems to be a fairly unspectacular picture of some fields and houses. However, close inspection reveals it to show some important sites of Forest's history that have never been seen before in a photograph. The picture was taken from the top of the Town Arms by the side of Trent Bridge on London Road, looking back across the Meadows. The field in the right foreground was known as Arkwright's Field, a portion of which was donated to Nottingham Forest in 1890 for the construction of the Town Ground. This photo shows the last remnants of that ground. Along the right side of the field is a drainage ditch and a bridge is still visible over it. This was constructed to allow Forest fans access from Bathley Street to the ground. From the end of this bridge you can also see a raised brick pavement which was put down outside the stand behind the goal to save fans from standing in a muddy field while entering and leaving the ground. This then gives a good idea of where the pitch actually was. The construction work starting in the far corner of the field is the building of Turney Street which still runs between the buildings of the bus depot that now occupies the site on Bunbury Street.

Above is the only known match photograph from inside the Town Ground. The houses in the background are by what is now Turney Street. Below is a photo showing the current bus depot in the distance where the Town Ground stand once stood. In 1897 Nottingham became a city and the ground was re-named The City Ground. When the club moved over the river in 1898 it was voted to retain the name and so the club's current stadium is actually the second City Ground.

NOTES ON SPORTS.

The most important meeting the League has ever held took place last evening at Sunderland. There was an attendance representative of all the leading football clubs, the League delegates present being Mr. J. J. Bentley (Bolton Wanderers), in the chair, Messrs. Lockett (secretary), Sutcliffe (Burnley), J. Marr (Sunderland), G. B. Ramsey (Aston Villa), J. Coe (Accrington), T. Mitchell (Blackburn Rovers), C. Grimes (Darwen), F. Dewhurst (Preston North End), E. Browne (Notts. County), Morley (Derby County), R. Molyneaux (Everton), Councillor Falby (Stoke), J. H. Addisbrook (Wolverhampton Wanderers), and Louis Ford (West Bromwich Albion). There was also a large number of representatives of outside clubs in attendance.

The first business was the selection of clubs to fill up the six vacancies necessary to bring up the first-class League to sixteen clubs. Application was made by West Bromwich Albion, which club was at once elected on the ground of having won the English Cup. Applications were then made on behalf of Accrington, Darwen, Stoke, Small Heath, Sheffield Wednesday, Newton Heath, Burton Swifts, Walsall Town Swifts, Notts. Forest, Sheffield United, Middlesbrough Ironopolis, and Newcastle East End.

After representatives had been heard in support of different clubs, the members proceeded to the election, with the result that

    Sheffield Wednesday
    Notts. Forest
    Accrington
    Stoke
    Newton Heath

were included in the League, which now consists of

Sunderland	Notts. County
Preston North End	Derby County
Bolton Wanderers	Stoke
Blackburn Rovers	West Bromwich Albion
Everton	Accrington
Aston Villa	Sheffield Wednesday
Wolverhampton Wanderers	Notts. Forest
Burnley	Newton Heath

FOOTBALL.

THE LEAGUE CHAMPIONSHIP.
FIRST DIVISION.

The following are the results in this competition up to date :—

	Played.	Won.	Lost.	Drawn.	For	Agst.	Pts.
Aston Villa	3	3	0	0	7	1	6
Sheffield Wednesday	2	2	0	0	6	2	4
W'hampton Wan	2	2	0	0	5	2	4
Preston North E.	2	2	0	0	4	2	4
Sunderland	2	1	0	1	8	3	3
Bolton Wanderers	2	1	0	1	8	3	3
Derby County	2	1	1	0	4	5	2
Blackburn Rovrs	2	1	1	0	6	7	2
Stoke	2	1	1	0	5	6	2
Notts. Forest	2	0	1	1	5	6	1
Notts. County	2	0	1	1	2	3	1
Newton Heath	2	0	1	1	4	5	1
Everton	2	0	1	1	3	6	1
Burnley	2	0	1	1	1	4	1
West Brom. Albn.	2	0	2	0	1	4	0
Accrington	2	0	2	0	2	11	0

FOREST v. STOKE.

Forest played their first League match at home on Saturday afternoon in the presence of 7,000 spectators. Stoke were their opponents, and although the weather was a bit too warm for football, a capital was seen.

Stoke, having won the toss, set Forest to play with the sun in their eyes, and Higgins kicked off. The preliminary passes were quickly stopped by Procter, but a bad kick by Clare sent the ball over the line. From the throw-in the visitors got the ball well up the field, and Dunn sent it flying across the mouth of the goal. Stoke were back again almost immediately, but Procter sent a long shot wide of the goal. A bit of brilliant passing between the Forest left-wingers brought the first round of applause from the crowd, who cheered a minute later as the "reds" dashed off into the right corner, where McCallum unfortunately fouled the ball.

[previous page] The Forest team for the 1892 FA Cup semi-final which lost to West Bromwich Albion after two replays.

[above] The vote which admitted Forest into the Football League and the first League table.

[opposite] Programme for the Forest at Aston Villa FA Cup tie in 1895.

NAMES AND POSITIONS OF PLAYERS.

THE ONLY OFFICIAL CARD.

Notts Forest v. Aston Villa,

(English Cup, 3rd Round)

AT PERRY BARR, MARCH 2ND, 1895.

NOTTS FOREST.

Referee—Mr. J. Lewis.　　　　Colours—Red Shirts and Blue Knicks.

D. ALLSOP
(11st.8)

A. RITCHIE　　　　　　　　　A. SCOTT (Capt.)
(12st.)　　　　　　　　　　　(12st.10)

P. McCRACKEN　　J. McPHERSON　　A. STEWART.
(12st.2)　　　　　(11st.9)　　　　　(11st.)

A. CARNELLY　　　　F. R. FORMAN
(11st.9)

H. PIKE　　　　　　T. ROSE　　　　　T. McINNES
(11st.12)　　　　　(11st.7)　　　　　(12st.7)

ASTON VILLA.

SMITH　　　　J. DEVEY　　　　C. ATHERSMITH
　　　　　　　(11st.9)　　　　　(10st.11)

D. HODGETTS　　　　　　　　R. CHATT
(14st.)　　　　　　　　　　　(12st.4)

G. RUSSELL　　　J. COWAN　　　　F. BURTON
(11st.2)　　　　(11st.10)　　　　(11st.7)

J. WELFORD　　　　　　　　ELLIOTT
(13st.6)

WILKES

COPYRIGHT—ONE PENNY.　　　Colours—Sky Blue and Claret.

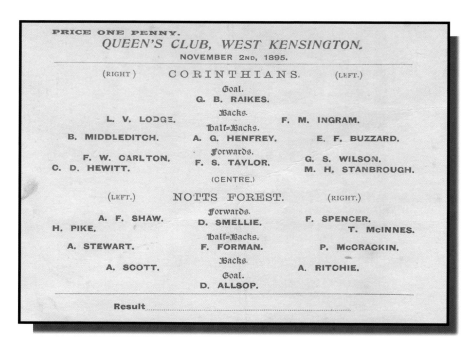

PRICE ONE PENNY.
QUEEN'S CLUB, WEST KENSINGTON.
NOVEMBER 2ND, 1895.

(RIGHT) **CORINTHIANS.** (LEFT.)

Goal.
G. B. RAIKES.

Backs.
L. V. LODGE.   F. M. INGRAM.

Half=Backs.
B. MIDDLEDITCH.   A. G. HENFREY.   E. F. BUZZARD.

Forwards.
F. W. CARLTON.   F. S. TAYLOR.   G. S. WILSON.
C. D. HEWITT.   M. H. STANBROUGH.

(CENTRE.)

(LEFT.) **NOTTS FOREST.** (RIGHT.)

Forwards.
A. F. SHAW.   D. SMELLIE.   F. SPENCER.
H. PIKE.   T. McINNES.

Half=Backs.
A. STEWART.   F. FORMAN.   P. McCRACKIN.

Backs.
A. SCOTT.   A. RITCHIE.

Goal.
D. ALLSOP.

Result ....

CRYSTAL PALACE.

FOOTBALL MATCH.
NOTTS FOREST v. DUNDEE.
Easter Monday, April 19th, 1897.

NOTTS FOREST.

Colours—Red.

Goal.
X
MARTIN.

RIGHT.   Backs.   LEFT.
X   X
RITCHIE.   SCOTT.

Half-Backs.
X   X   X
J. FORMAN.   McPHERSON.   WRAGG.

Forwards.
X   X   X   X   X
F. R. FORMAN.   Ar. CAPES.   Ad. CAPES.   RICHARDS.   McINNES.

○

Forwards.
X   X   X   X   X
SMITH.   WILLOCKS.   DEVLIN.   CLARK.   ALLAN.

Half-Backs.
X   X   X
KEILLER.   McARTHUR.   STORMONT.

LEFT.   Backs.   RIGHT.
X   X
BURGESS.   KELSO or HAMILTON.

Goal.
X
HILLMAN.

DUNDEE.

Referee—MR. W. J. WILSON.

Frank and Fred Forman both played for England in all three home internationals, a record that stood until the Charlton brothers matched it in the 1960s.

The Maypole Yard Hotel became Forest's headquarters after the informal arrangements at the Clinton Arms. The building is still there off Clumber Street.

Maypole Hotel,

NOTTINGHAM.

HEADQUARTERS OF

NOTTM. FOREST

LUNCHEONS, TEAS,

AND BEDS

FOR

FOOTBALL CLUBS.

[opposite] Images from the 1898 FA Cup semi-final with Southampton. Referee Lewis had been in charge for the quarter-final and both games against Southampton in the semi-final. As these cuttings show, the first game ended 1-1 before Forest prevailed in a snowstorm, 2-0, in the replay at Bramall Lane. Lewis was criticised in some quarters but the whispers of a demonstration at the final were unfounded, even though he was in charge yet again.

HOW THE MATCH WAS PLAYED

NOTES BY THE WAY

A SENSATIONAL OPENING

FOREST SCORE IN THREE MINUTES

"SO'TON" REPLY IN TWENTY

BOTH FROM FREE KICKS

SCENE ON THE GROUND.

The gates were not opened until two o'clock, but at that time the entrances in John-street were thronged by a crowd of excited people, and along the approaches to the ground was a continuous stream of pedestrians all hastening to the scene of the encounter, whilst already the thoroughfares were animated with a line of hurrying vehicles discharging their eager freight. Bramall-lane ground is in no sense a picturesque enclosure. Indeed, environed as it is by commonplace houses with what little turf there ever was on the football pitch looking like a frayed out carpet, and with a murky atmosphere overhead, through which the sickly sun failed to penetrate, it presented a very unattractive, although, certainly, a business-like aspect. The accommodation for the public is, however, of a most satisfactory character, and no doubt the whole of the 25,000 spectators were able to obtain, without inconvenience, a

PLUCKY FIGHT BY SOUTH-AMPTON.

GAME PLAYED IN A GALE.

ALLSOP SAVES A PENALTY.

For the first time in the history of the club Forest have reached the final stage of the struggle for the English Cup. On four previous occasions they have been semi-finalists. Will they now win the Cup? That good old Forester, "Sam" Widdowson, was in London on Thursday, and seemed more enthusiastic than anyone over the result. The truth is that he celebrates his birthday on April 16th, and that being the date of the final he sees visions of two important events coming off together. Of course, the second event is the winning of the English Cup by the Forest team. I hope the players will oblige. They have had nothing to spare in the semi-final either at Sheffield or London. There were those who thought that the tie with Southampton was a "good" thing for Forest, but the Southerners have turned out sturdy foemen, and no one who has seen the two matches will cavil at me for offering them very hearty congratulations. They have fought splendidly, and have shown beyond all question that they are not inferior to at least half the teams in the First Division of the League. For indomitable pluck and perseverance they would be difficult to beat, and coupled with this earnestness is thoroughly good-class football. There wasn't a tremendous crowd to see the fight, but there was such a lot of weather about that the gathering of 16,800—those are the official figures—must be reckoned a thoroughly satisfactory one. Snowstorms were experienced at intervals throughout the day, and from early morning it was cold—bitterly cold. The Southampton club had reluctantly to leave out Farrell, whose absence necessitated a rearrangement of the forward rank, Buchanan playing centre, and Brown being outside right, with Stevens as partner. Southampton had the good luck to win the toss, and with the wind blowing a gale from goal to

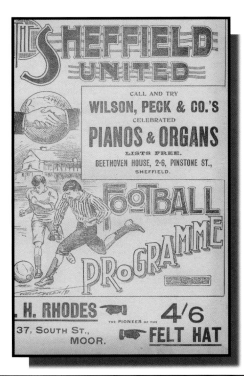

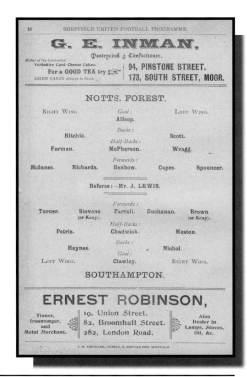

NOTTS. FOREST.

| RIGHT WING. | | Goal : Allsop. | | LEFT WING. |

| | | Backs : | | |
| | Ritchie. | | Scott. | |

| | | Half-Backs : | | |
| | Forman. | McPherson. | Wragg. | |

| | | Forwards : | | |
| McInnes. | Richards. | Benbow. | Capes. | Spouncer. |

Referee :—Mr. J. LEWIS.

| | | Forwards : | | |
| Turner. | Stevens (or Keay). | Farrell. | Buchanan. | Brown (or Keay). |

| | | Half-Backs : | | |
| | Petrie. | Chadwick. | Meston. | |

| | | Backs : | | |
| | Haynes. | | Nichol. | |

| | | Goal : | | |
| LEFT WING. | | Clawley. | | RIGHT WING. |

SOUTHAMPTON.

NOTTM. FOREST FOOTBALL CLUB.

1864-1898.

The appearance of the Forest club in the final stage of the competition for the English Cup is an event unparalleled in the history of the club, and therefore the occasion is one on which one may well look back over the career of an organisation which takes rank among the oldest football clubs of the country. To begin with it would be well to give just a general idea as to the formation and growth of the club.

STORY OF THE CLUB'S PROGRESS.

The Forest Football Club was born so long ago that there exists some uncertainty as to the exact time of its formation, but so far as can be gathered there appears every reason to believe that the club was founded in the year 1864. The story of the start-

FOOTBALL.
THE CUP FINAL

DISCONTENTED SOUTHERNERS

TALK OF A DEMONSTRATION AGAINST THE "REDS."

"Wanderer," writing in to-day's "Sportsman," says:—"There is every expectation that the attendance on Saturday at the Crystal Palace will exceed all record, in fact, accommodation is being made for 80,000 onlookers. About another 1,600 ring seats (unreserved) will be provided, at half-a-crown each, an additional circle being found possible. There has been some talk about a "demonstration" against Mr. Lewis and the Notts. Forest F.C., but I sincerely trust there will be no such folly committed. As for the 'reds,' how are they to be blamed, though it is impossible not to sympathise with the Southampton men in their hard luck? With regard to the offer of a bicycle to the first goal-getter, I trust that this inducement to selfish play will be dealt with as "captain" Wreford-Brown did at Glasgow, viz., the cycle put up for 'auction' and the sum realised divided among the professional contestants."

FOOTBALL THE NEWS

NOTTINGHAM, SATURDAY, APRIL 16, 1898.

THE CUP FINAL AT THE CRYSTAL PALACE.

SPECIAL ILLUSTRATED NUMBER.

Notts. Forest v. Derby County.

BRIEF NOTES AND PORTRAITS OF OFFICIALS AND PLAYERS.

OFFICERS OF THE FOREST CLUB.

Chairman—Mr W T Hancock.　　Hon. Sec.—Mr. H S Radford.　　Secretary—Mr H Hallam.

Early reports of Forest's history put the formation of the club at 1864.

J. Macpherson (Captain).   Adam Scott.   W. Wragg.   J. Iremonger.

Dennis Allsop.   Leonard Benbow.   Frank Forman.   Archibald Ritchie.

Chas. H. Richards.   A. Spouncer.   Arthur Capes.   Thomas McInnes.

The Forest side that lined up to face Derby in the 1898 FA Cup Final at Crystal Palace.

The only known photograph from the 1898 FA Cup Final. Forest players trot back to their half after scoring one of the goals in their 3-1 win.

FIRST DIVISION STRAGGLE

POSITIONS UP TO DATE

LEAGUE CHAMPIONSHIP

| 42 | 37 | 35 | 35 | 33 | 32 | 31 | 31 | 28 | 28 | 26 | 24 | 24 | 24 | 24 | 24 |

MONDAY, APRIL 18, 1898

CUP WINNERS' RETURN.

MIDLAND STATION : 8.10 P.M.

TO-NIGHT'S ARRANGEMENTS

TRIUMPHAL DRIVE THROUGH THE CITY

After the magnificent victory which the "reds" have gained they will doubtless have a great reception when they bring the Cup home to-night. The wonderful enthusiasm created by Saturday's triumph has abated just a little, but the return of the Foresters will be certain to cause a fresh outburst. The victorious eleven deserve as fine a greeting as any team ever did. The home coming bids fair to be worthy of the occasion. It will be a great day for men like McPherson, Scott, Ritchie, Allsop, and McInnes, who have served the club for a number of years, and can hardly hope to again find places in an English Cup winning team, and as for the players who have become associated with Forest recently, they all deserve the honour they have won for themselves. Frank Forman and Wragg in the half-back line, together with four dashing forwards like Richards, Benbow, Capes, and Spouncer, have all played in a manner worthy of the club. While yet young men they have reached the dizzy heights of football fame. There was no more pleasing sight at the Palace on Saturday than that of Benbow, as bold a little fellow as ever played football, coming out of the pavilion carrying the Cup in its case. Later on the trophy was to be seen on the front of the conveyance which took the "reds" away from the Palace, and those who go down to the Midland Station to-night will be sure to have a view of the great prize which Forest now hold. The arrangements for meeting the successful players are not of a particularly elaborate character, but the interest aroused by the wonderful performance of the team, and the anxiety of local football followers to show their appreciation of the victory, are certain to result in a demonstration so enthusiastic as to make the event one which will long live in the memories of Nottingham footballers.

The train by which the Foresters arrive in Nottingham to-night leaves St. Pancras at 5.40, and reaches Nottingham at ten minutes past eight.

[below] Even over a 100 years ago there were memorabilia opportunities from the Reds cup win. With what may be the first Forest collectable, Dilks & Co. produced this glass etching that commemorated the victory. It's thought that none survive to this day.

[next page] The brand new City Ground, pictured in September 1898. Forest moved into the 'new' City Ground in August 1898 with their opening fixture south of the Trent against Blackburn Rovers on September 3rd, a game which they lost 1-0. The new facilities were among the most modern available.

ENGLISH ASSOCIATION CUP.

FINAL TIE

AT THE CRYSTAL PALACE, APRIL 16th, 1898, BETWEEN

NOTTS. FOREST

AND

DERBY COUNTY,

THE FORMER BEING VICTORIOUS BY 3 GOALS TO 1.

Messrs. DILKS and CO., LIMITED, Chromo Printers, WARSER-GATE, NOTTINGHAM, have issued a very Attractive

PHOTO ENGRAVING

TO COMMEMORATE THIS EVENT.

IT IS DRAWN BY ONE OF THEIR SPECIAL ARTISTS ON THE SPOT.

An Illuminated Border with the Football Association Badge in gold and colour, and the Cup in silver.

SAMPLE (Size 20 by 15) POST FREE, 6 STAMPS.

SPECIAL QUOTATIONS FOR QUANTITIES.

The 20th Century...

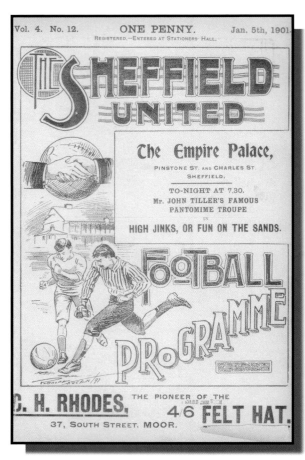

Linacre filled the Forest goal last Saturday in more senses than one, and almost alone saved his side from defeat by the Villa.

[left] Harry Linacre was one of Forest's best players in the early 1900s and played twice for England.

[previous pages] Forest fans make their way to The City Ground for a game in 1900. The back of the Main Stand enclosure is at the far left of the picture, a cricket game is in progress at Trent Bridge and the site of County Hall is just a wooded park.

[opposite] The 1901 contract of William Barnett, he played just two League games for the club.

Nottingham Forest Football Club.

Memorandum of the Terms of Engagement of

Colleslan Barnett

as Professional Football Player with the Nottingham Forest Football Club.

  The said player undertakes to play football as, when, and where directed by the Committee or Officials of the Nottingham Forest Football Club, and to sign the necessary Registration Forms as required by the English Association and the Football League, or such other ruling body as the said club may belong to. And further, the said player undertakes to conduct himself soberly and respectably, and to do all acts and things necessary to be in fit condition to play football, and to win each match in which he shall be selected to play.

  In consideration of these services the Forest Football Club agrees to pay to the said *Wm Barnett* as follows:

Ten shillings & 6ᵈ Per week, from *Sept 1st 1901* to *Apl 30th 1902*

& £2 (two pounds) Per week from *week when playing with the First Team in cup tie or League matches*

Failing the due fulfilment by the player of the conditions as above stated, the club may, at their option, withold the payment for any period which they may deem desirable.

      Signed, *B Hallam*

Witness
Co. R. Murray
May 6th 1901

NOTTS FOREST v. NEWCASTLE UNITED.
THE LEAGUE LEADERS BEATEN AT HOME.

THE KICK OFF.

AN UNLUCKY SLIP SPOILS A DANGEROUS FOREST RUN.

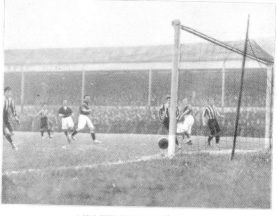

A NEAR THING FOR THE UNITEDS' GOAL.

THE UNITEDS CLEAR A CORNER.

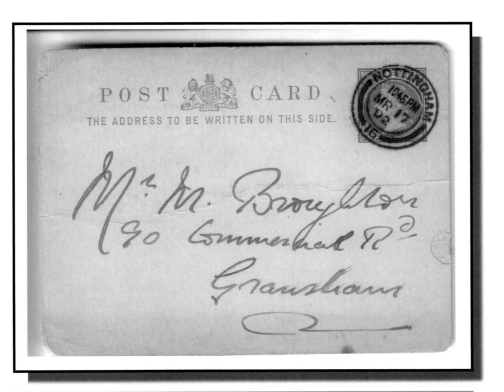

POST CARD

THE ADDRESS TO BE WRITTEN ON THIS SIDE.

Mr M. Broughton
90 Commercial Rd
Grantham

This late night post card was sent on Monday night asking Matt Broughton to play for Forest on Wednesday afternoon against Newcastle United. He made it on time to play on the right-wing during a 2-0 home defeat in 1902.

TELEPHONE 1382.

Nottingham Forest Football Club

SECRETARY:
H. HALLAM.

MAYPOLE YARD.
(DATE AS POST-MARK.)

Dear Matt
You are selected to play against Newcastle on Wednesday kick off 3.15 trusting you will be able to get off please wire me if unable to do so
Yours &c
H Hallam

NOTTINGHAM FOREST F.C.

CITY GROUND
NOTTINGHAM

Nottingham Forest are an old League club, dating from 1865, three years after the rival football combination of the lace city—Notts. The club that plays now on the City Ground, red-shirted and white-knickered, claims to have been the first to adopt the 'now general three-half-back system. It should be said, however, that this claim is also put forward on behalf of Turton. The referee's whistle was first used on the ground of the club in 1878, and in this connection it may be noted that S. W. Widdowson, the old Nottingham Forest International, brought out and registered shinguards in 1874.

Last season Nottingham Forest played 34 games in the First Division of the League, winning 14 of them and losing 13, whilst seven were left drawn. For the Forest 49 goals were scored and 47 against, leaving the club with 35 points as contrasted to the 42 which sufficed to secure the championship for Sheffield Wednesday. That grand forward—the finest inside-left of the day—Arthur Grenville Morris—got as many as five-and-twenty of the Forest goals, which works out to more than all the rest of his colleagues put together. Linacre and he only missed a match apiece, while Iremonger played in the whole series of the League games. It was hardly a glorious season for Nottingham Forest, though the team fairly kept to its position of the preceding year, and came up in the table a bit towards the close. Though they have given fine football displays at times in this competition, it is a singular thing that the Forest Club have never got into the first three of the teams engaged in any year.

When the Forest met the Old Etonians in 1879 in the Cup tourney they had John Sands in goal, who, it will be recollected, gained a cap against Wales in the following year. Charles J. Caborn made a splendid back, and the halves were the brothers Edward and Walter Luntley. In front were M. Holroyd, A. J. Bates, Arthur Goodyer, and Sam Weller Widdowson, both of the latter subsequently playing against Scotland. E. Earp was absent from the tie through illness.

Amongst the earliest players for the club were C. F. Daft, elder brother of the famous Richard Daft, who bought the players a dozen red flannel caps in which to perform, red from that day becoming the colour of the club. Games between Nottingham Forest and Notts. commenced in 1866.

In Mr. H. S. Radford the Forest have had a good divisional representative on the Council of the Football Association. It was with the club, for which he has done many years admirable service, that Mr. Radford first got into touch with football. When he was secretary to the Forest he was elected an auditor of the Football League, and in 1898 became a member of the Management Committee. The present secretary, Mr. H. Hallam, is a rare good worker, as is also the respected honorary treasurer. Mr. T. G. Howitt, while the committee over which Mr. W. T. Hancock so ably presides, though larger than that of most clubs, is very active.

The famous brethren, Fred and Frank Forman,

a tea service from H. J. Linacre, the Forest goalkeeper, who is a cousin of the Formans. The Forest executive are splendid employers when players are loyal to the club and game.

James Iremonger is to have a big benefit early in the new year, and the present captain of the Forest team well deserves the recognition. He has played for the club for ten seasons, and often took charge before Forman's retirement. He is a resolute and fearless back, splendid in any emergency. He has played for England and acquitted himself well. He is six-and-twenty, and although born in Yorkshire has practically lived his life and learned his football in the neighbourhood of Nottingham. Iremonger did not signalise his advent to the captaincy of the Forest team quite as he would have wished. He is noted for his nerve, and on that account he has for a long time always been entrusted with the Forest penalty kicks. One was awarded to the "Reds" in the second half of the League match against Liverpool at the opening of this season. Morris was running close in, and appeared certain to score, when Dunlop brought him down unfairly. There was never the least question as to the decision of the referee on the point, and Iremonger prepared to take the kick. He, however, sent very wide. But he rarely makes a miss of this kind.

H. J. Linacre.

Nottingham Forest won the Association Cup in 1898, beating Derby County by 3 to 1, and prior to this appeared many times in the semi-final stage, without, however, reaching the last round of all.

A spectator who was present in 1878 at an Association Cup match between Notts. and the Forest says that so little interest was then taken in the competition that the crowd paying for admission only numbered 500, while 250 would perhaps be good figures for those who occupied free seats. Now a good Cup game between the two famous Nottingham clubs would draw a crowd of well on to a hundred times as many, and in the 1902 semi-final of the Cup, when Nottingham Forest met Southampton, 20,000 people were in attendance, and the receipts ran up to £1,400. Last year the gate receipts on the Forest ground ran up to £6,416, and £3,867 was paid away in players' wages. The club ended up its season with a credit balance of over £1,200.

have done splendid service in their day for the Forest. Frank played at centre-half or England against Scotland at Birmingham as late as May in 1902, but, though his side did not lose, the famous old International was obviously past his best, and some folks rather wondered why he was chosen, good man as he once was. This famous and much-esteemed player may now be said to have virtually given up professional football, though he has signed a form for the Forest in case he might be wanted sometime—which appears to be very imminent. In signing the form, Forman said that he would never play football for anybody but the Forest; he did not want any payment, and had signed simply and purely to assist the club if he were needed. In lieu of the benefit which Forman refused last year, a very handsome present, consisting of a silver rose-bowl and substantial cheque, was made to him when he was married last June. Other gifts to the famous half-back were three handsome silver cups from Mr. T. Clamp, a vice-president of the Forest Club, and

Nottingham Forest to-day have almost a full team of Southern Leaguers, the following players for the "Reds" having all at one time or other in their career taken part in Southern football—Calvey, Morris, Sugden, Newbigging Craig, Jones, Innes, Henderson, Davies, and Griffiths. Swindon has been a fine hunting ground for the Foresters. Then Shearman, the ex-Shepherd's Bush amateur, who played first for the Forest this season in the Sheffield Wednesday match last Saturday, and scored the only goal obtained by the side, is another promising capture from the South Country, being a most active forward.

Harry Linacre is a reliable goalkeeper, with a big reach, and precious hard to beat. He will be an International before long. Craig, the big Scotchman, who came from West Ham at the beginning of last season, makes a fine and fittingly stalwart partner for Iremonger at back, with young Jones, one of the recruits from Swindon, who looks like being a useful find, to fall back upon.

It cannot, however, be said that the half-backs have come up to expectations, and, so far, what used to be considered the Forest's strong department, has been very weak. Neither Warren, Innes, nor Crawford have matured as desired, and without a strong, forceful personality at centre-half the line has been very unimpressionable. Forward, the terrible falling away of Calvey has given the club considerable trouble, and it has been well for it that it had a man of the unusual calibre of Morris at command. However, the engagement of Shearman

of last season, makes a fine and fittingly stalwart partner for Iremonger at back, with young Jones, one of the recruits from Swindon, who looks like being a useful find, to fall back upon.

It cannot, however, be said that the half-backs have come up to expectations, and so far, what used to be considered the Forest's strong department, has been very weak. Neither Warren, Innes, nor Crawford have matured as desired, and without a strong, forceful personality at centre-half the line has been very unimpressionable. Forward, the terrible falling away of Calvey has given the club considerable trouble, and it has been well for it that it had a man of the unusual calibre of Morris at command. However, the engagement of Shearman is expected to remedy the deficiency of the old Millwall man, and although Davies, late of Swindon, is on the small side, either he or Turner, the old Crouch End Vampire, should fill the place on the extreme right of the line with credit to it. Spouncer is playing as well, if not better, than ever he did, and Sugden if light for his position, is both clever and useful in front of goal, so that with a smart attack and a big, powerful defence the team only requires a stronger intermediate line to fulfil the highest hopes of its supporters.

Last season the Reserves figured with conspicuous success in the Notts. and District League, but this season finds them engaged amid more imposing surroundings, namely, the Midland Counties League, in which up to date they have done remarkably well. On the opening day of the season they paid a barren visit to Bramall Lane, but on the Saturday following they got a point at Grimsby, and on the 12th September drew with Chesterfield at Chesterfield, following this up seven days later by beating Doncaster Rovers, who took part last season in Division II., the match transpiring at Doncaster. When Sheffield Wednesday came to Nottingham the "Reds" had the vilest of luck, as after scoring the first goal the "Blades" had had against them thus far, they lost a goal and a point in the last moments of the game. Against Newark and Grimsby at home, however, they won easily, and this morning stood fourth in the table, with nine points from eight matches and a goal balance of 14—10—no mean performance considering the importance of the step taken and the calibre of the opponents the Reserves have had to meet.

A DETERMINED ATTACK.

Grenville Morris on the attack against Derby at The City Ground

[opposite] In July 1904 a fairground ride at the Midlands Industrial Exhibition caught fire. The flames spread to the back of the Main Stand at The City Ground and gutted the building.

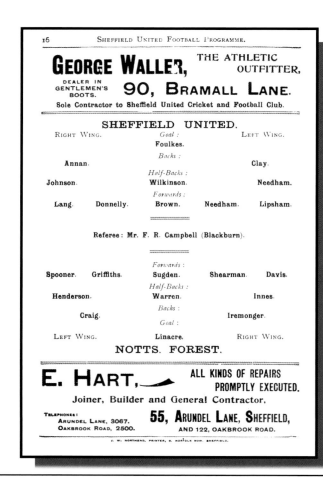

SHEFFIELD UNITED.

RIGHT WING.		Goal :		LEFT WING.
		Foulkes.		
		Backs :		
Annan.				Clay.
		Half-Backs :		
Johnson.		Wilkinson.		Needham.
		Forwards :		
Lang.	Donnelly.	Brown.	Needham.	Lipsham.

Referee : Mr. F. R. Campbell (Blackburn).

		Forwards :		
Spooner.	Griffiths.	Sugden.	Shearman.	Davis.
		Half-Backs :		
Henderson.		Warren.		Innes.
		Backs :		
	Craig.			Iremonger.
		Goal :		
LEFT WING.		Linacre.		RIGHT WING.

NOTTS. FOREST.

Forest took an adventurous trip in the summer of 1905 when they sailed to South America for nine games in Argentina.

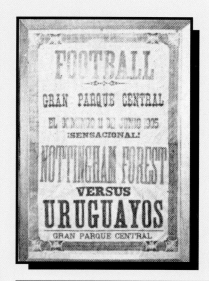

The 1905-06 team picture was taken in the players' sunday best suits. Back row, left to right; George Lessons, Harry Linacre, Walter Dudley, George Wolfe, H. Rothery, James Iremonger, Robert Norris (trainer). Middle row, left to right; Charles Craggs, Enoch West, William Shearman, Grenville Morris, Alfred Spouncer. Front row, left to right; Edwin Hughes, Jack Armstrong, George Maltby.

Despite having a strong team, Forest somehow managed to get relegated for the first time in their history. Jack Armstrong is still seventh in the all-time list of Forest appearances (460), the potent strike-force of Morris and West netted 34 goals, and Welsh international Hughes bolstered the defence. The bulk of this team was retained and bounced back to the First Division at the first attempt.

GALLAHER'S CIGARETTES.

A. GRENVILLE MORRIS,
NOTTS FOREST, 1909-10.

A. GRENVILLE-MORRIS

26 A. G. MORRIS, Notts Forest.

Packed with *Singleton & Cole's* HIGH GRADE CIGARETTES

OGDEN'S CIGARETTES.

A. G. MORRIS.

Thirty-seven goals from Enoch West and Grenville Morris propelled Forest to the Second Division championship in 1906-07.

PROMINENT FOOTBALLERS.

H. J. WEST,
NOTTS FOREST.

Double event wanted.

"You've well earned it, my lad, and I hope you'll soon win another."

[Forest have won premier honours in the Midland Section, and expect to continue the good work when the supplementary league gets going.]

The Second Division champions in 1907. Back row, left to right; George Needham, Edwin Hughes, Walter Dudley, George Wolfe, Harry Linacre, George Maltby, Robert Norris (trainer). Front row, left to right; William Hooper, Thomas Marrison, Arthur Green, Grenville Morris, Enoch West, Jack Armstrong.

PROMINENT FOOTBALLERS.

J. ARMSTRONG.
NOTTS FOREST.

PROMINENT FOOTBALLERS.

W. DUDLEY,

PROMINENT FOOTBALLERS.

GIBSON,

PROMINENT FOOTBALLERS.

W. HOOPER,
NOTTS FOREST.

PROMINENT FOOTBALLERS.

G. H. MALTBY,
NOTTS FOREST.

PROMINENT FOOTBALLERS.

G. WOLFE,

A selection of Forest players from the Taddy & Co. set of Prominent Footballers.

Taken from a recently discovered glass plate negative, this clear copy of the 1912-13 team shows a Forest side that finished 17th in the Second Division. Back row, left to right; unknown trainer, Walter Dudley, George Needham, John Hanna, Joe Mercer, Robert Reid, Bob Marsters (secretary), Robert Norris (trainer). Middle row, left to right; Thomas Gibson, Harry Jones, Grenville Morris, Harold Lemoine, Robert Firth. Front row, left to right; Alfred Fisher, Jack Armstrong, John Derrick, Frederick Banks, J. B. Ford.

"Yah! Turn him off!"

[The professional footballer just now is catching it hot because he is not enlisting, and those who look on are also being bitterly jeered at.]

"If you want to come and join us do it soon."

[Recruits have come in well for the Footballers' Battalion, but there are still many gaps to be filled, and it is hoped the efforts that are being made in Nottingham will have fruitful results.]

[opposite] After the war broke out in 1914 the sports press joined the propaganda machine to get both players and fans to sign up for military action.

[above] Special footballers battalions were formed during the First World War but players also turned out for 'regular' army teams. Here is the Middlesex Regiment which included Foresters Harold Iremonger, Thomas Gibson and Joe Mercer (all on back row).

[left] John Derrick in his army uniform, was able to come back and watch Forest play while on leave from duty.

The final war-time season, 1918-19, culminated with the midlands champions (Forest) playing-off against the northern champions (Everton). The home and away tie has in the years after the event been referred to as the Victory Shield, though this seems to have been a recent invention. No reports from the time mention such a trophy, in fact the trophy that was awarded is the League Championship trophy, the exact same one which Forest also won in 1977-78 and 1997-98. Thus becoming the only team to win the same trophy three times, each for a different competition. Forest drew 0-0 and home then won 1-0 at Goodison Park to take the trophy.

Everton in the Offing

"I reckon I know what you've set your mind on."

(Forest, whose Easter fare on Monday consists of the return game with Notts, are eager awaiting the coming of Everton.)

NOTTM. FOREST F.C.

OFFICIAL CARD OF THE MATCH.

League Championship Match—NOTTM. FOREST v EVERTON

(Champions Midland Section) (Champions Lancashire Section)

City Ground, Nottingham, May 10, 1919

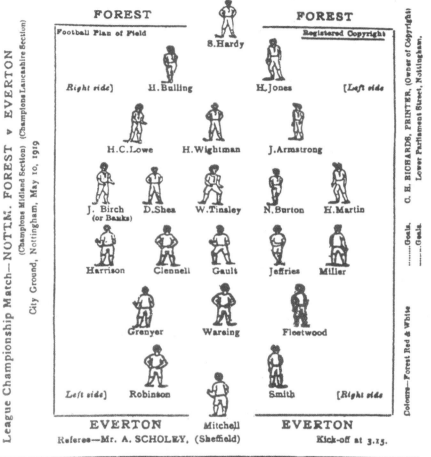

FOREST   FOREST

Football Plan of Field   Registered Copyright

S.Hardy

Right side)   H. Bulling   H. Jones   [Left side

H.C.Lowe   H. Wightman   J.Armstrong

J. Birch (or Banks)   D.Shea   W.Tinsley   N.Burton   H.Martin

Harrison   Clennell   Gault   Jeffries   Miller

Grenyer   Wareing   Fleetwood

Left side)   Robinson   Smith   [Right side

EVERTON   Mitchell   EVERTON

Referee—Mr. A. SCHOLEY, (Sheffield)   Kick-off at 3.15.

C. H. RICHARDS, PRINTER, (Owner of Copyright)
Lower Parliament Street, Nottingham.

......Goals.
......Goals.

Colours—Forest Red & White

The 1920s

[above] Two unidentified players pose in front of the River End stand, the original name for the Trent End.

[below] Sid Gibson receives some rudimentary treatment in the early 1920s.

The 1922 Second Division champions, complete with winner's shield. Back row, left to right: Montgomery (trainer), R. Atkinson, unknown, Jack Armstrong, unknown, unknown, J. Thom, Percy Barratt, unknown, Alfred Bennett. Middle row, left to right; Bob Marsters (secretary / manager), Jack Belton, Robert Parker, Harry Jones, Sidney Harrold, Patrick Nelis, Henry Martin. Front row, left to right; Sid Gibson, Jack Spaven, Fred Parker, Noah Burton. Unidentified players on this picture are likely to include Boyman, Ashmore and Dennis.

NOTTINGHAM FOREST FOOTBALL CLUB.

REVENUE ACCOUNT, SEASON 1922 - 1923.

EXPENDITURE

	£ s. d.	£ s. d.	£ s. d.
Dr. Balance brought forward		1143 18 2	
Wages and Salaries	11151 0 0		
Transfer Fees	3120 0 0		
		14271 0 0	
Match Expenses (home)	1481 12 3		
do. (away) (including Training and Travelling)	2251 18 5		
do. Reserves	341 14 4		
		4025 5 0	
Maintenance of Ground	2102 1 11		
Rent, Gas and Water	180 4 4		
Rates, Taxes and Insurances ...	441 11 3		
Printing, Posting and Advertising ...	266 12 8		
Subscriptions, Donations and League Levies	149 15 3		
Interest and Bank Commission ...	136 3 6		
Outfits and Football requirements ...	174 15 10		
Watch Fund	100 0 0		
Medical attendance and Sundries ...	212 12 3		
		3763 17 0	
Benefit Account		866 8 11	
		£24070 9 1	

RECEIPTS

	£ s. d.	£ s. d.	£ s. d.
Match Receipts	27103 0 5		
Less Tax	5247 13 3		
	21855 7 2		
Less percentage to Visitors ...	3336 18 7		
	18518 8 7		
Plus percentage received ...	2905 5 5		
		21423 14 0	
Subscriptions (less tax) ...		1847 7 10	
Sundry Ground Receipts ...		280 2 6	
		23551 4 4	
Dr. Balance carried forward ...		519 4 9	
		£24070 9 1	

I have examined the Accounts of the Nottingham Forest Football Club, together with the books and vouchers relating thereto, and hereby certify the above statement to be correct.

C. K. SWANN, Auditor.

1 Waldeck Road, Nottingham.
June 22nd, 1923.

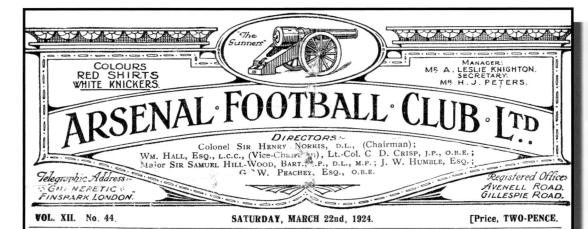

COLOURS
RED SHIRTS
WHITE KNICKERS.

"The Gunners"

MANAGER:
Mr A. LESLIE KNIGHTON.
SECRETARY:
Mr H. J. PETERS.

ARSENAL · FOOTBALL · CLUB · LTD.

DIRECTORS:—
Colonel SIR HENRY NORRIS, D.L., (Chairman);
WM. HALL, ESQ., L.C.C., (Vice-Chairman), Lt.-Col. C. D. CRISP, J.P., O.B.E.;
Major SIR SAMUEL HILL-WOOD, BART., J.P., D.L., M.P.; J. W. HUMBLE, ESQ.;
G. W. PEACHEY, ESQ., O.B.E.

Telegraphic Address:—
GUNNERETIC
FINSPARK, LONDON.

Registered Office:
AVENELL ROAD.
GILLESPIE ROAD.

VOL. XII. No. 44. SATURDAY, MARCH 22nd, 1924. [Price, TWO-PENCE.

OUR EDITORIAL NOTE

BY "THE GUNNERS' MATE."

As Others See Us.

I am bound to confess to a feeling of disappointment when I saw the points "go west" at Nottingham last Saturday. The brilliant form shown by our team against Liverpool and later against Aston Villa had certainly given me reason to hope for victory. But it was not to be. And let me say quite frankly that we did not deserve to lose. That is my own opinion and is in the opinion of "Impressionist," one of the leading critics on the "Athletic News" staff. He writes, "All round the Arsenal were the better craftsmen, the adaptable masters of the impish ball. This much was evidenced at intervals in the first period, and forcibly driven home throughout the second half, when the Forest became reduced to a medley of desperate concern. . . . . . That the Forest earned the points, I cannot admit." This unbiassed criticism may be cold sort of comfort but it does give us some encouragement to hope for brighter days. I hope we will meet with better fortune to-day when we play the return match with the Forest, whom we have every reason to regard as a very strong and determined lot and one that will go all out to the last minute.

Our New Helper.

I am certain you will all be delighted to see Andrew Neil in our colours to-day. His reputation in top-class football is well known at Highbury and elsewhere. For two seasons he has been one of the chief factors in keeping Brighton and Hove near the top of the Southern Section of the Third Division and for their successful exploits in the Cup competition. It is also common knowledge that his services were sought after by many First Division sides and I have not the slightest doubt that Neil will demonstrate to our directors and to Manager Knighton that their bargain was a good one. Curiously enough, Neil was born at Kilmarnock, from which town Ramsey came to us recently, though he, by the way, was born in Glasgow. Neil came under the notice of Charlie Webb, the Brighton Manager when he was assisting Tottenham, and, so to speak, has made rapid progress during his association with the Brighton club. He is still a mere youth, stands 5-ft. 7½-inches high and weighs eleven stone. We hope he will long wear the red jersey with credit to himself and complete satisfaction to the club. My reference to Ramsey above reminds me that I saw the statement recently that "Ramsey" was classed as one of Scotland's "Premier" forwards. I think the joke a good one but it is happily, also a statement of fact.

The Foresters.

We are pleased to extend a very hearty welcome to the Forest to-day, though many of the older enthusiasts will regret the probable absence of the great goalkeeper, Sam Hardy. He was always a great London favourite but in Bennett he has a fine deputy and the Forest defence is one of the most virile in the country. So, too, is their dashing half-back line, in which we will see the old Forest stalwart, Belton, and the dashing auburn haired Morgan, who, on his day, is a particularly powerful force. In the forward line there are several men of note, of whom Martin, the outside left, is probably the best known. You all remember this tall dark speedy left winger when he used to partner George Holley in the Sunderland team. Increasing years

A selection of the Forest players included in the mammoth set of Pinnace cards issued in cigarette packets during the early 1920s. Over 1,500 players were included.

A couple of informal player shots taken in the garden behind the Main Stand. Above, the flat caps are modelled, below it's Jack Armstrong (far left) and Walter Tinsley (far right) showing off their latest suits.

[opposite] The official list of players insured for the 1967-27 season.

Name and Address of Player or Trainer Insured.	Date of Commencement of Liability.	Remarks.
Barratt Percy	14 Aug 1926	
Bolton J	"	
Bennett A	"	
Burton H	"	
Dexter A	"	
Galloway R	"	
Gibson J G	"	
Hampson E	"	
Hodgkinson V A	"	
Jones C	"	
Langford L	"	
Lynas R J L	"	
Marsden H	"	
Morgan J G	"	
Price E C	"	
Reed E	"	
Saxton J	"	
Stocks C W	"	
Taylor J	"	
Thompson W P	"	
Townsend A H	"	
Walker D C	"	
Wallace R S 23	"	

The City Ground has gradually been improved and expanded over the 111 years that Forest have played there. This late 1920s picture shows the expanded Bridgford End as a large earth bank that served as terracing. Before that there were just eight rows of wooden steps.

FOREST DRAW WITH BOLTON

A ding-dong Cup-tie   Both Manchesters win

ARSENAL OUT   DERBY'S SCORER

Trouble at Meadow Lane after the draw

Nottingham Forest	2	Bolton Wanderers	2	
(Stocks, Burton.)		(Butler 2.)		
Manchester City	6	*Clapton Orient	1	
(Johnson 3, Roberts, Browell, Hicks.)		(Cock.)		
Manchester United	2	*Fulham	1	
(McPherson, Smith.)		(Pape.)		
Swansea	2	Arsenal	1	
(Thompson, Fowler.)		(Mackie.)		

THE REDS' RECOMPENSE

"We're pleased to meet you at last, Mr. Fat-Gate"
(And, on top of the big receipts at Bolton. there should be another fine attendance on Monday.)

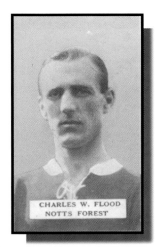

CHARLES W. FLOOD
NOTTS FOREST

As Forest languished in the Second Division for much of the 1920s and 1930s it was the occasional FA Cup run which made the most headlines. In 1926 they battled Bolton Wanderers through two replays in the quarter-finals before losing 1-0. The six FA Cup games brought the Reds some much-needed revenue.

[next page] Two years later, still stuck in the Second Division, Forest had another famous cup run. This time they reached the fifth round (beating Derby in a fourth round replay in front of a record City Ground crowd of over 35,000) where they faced the holders, Cardiff City. Despite going a goal down at The City Ground Forest shocked the football world by winning 2-1. The run eventually ended in the quarter finals again, this time with a 3-0 loss at Sheffield United.

A GREAT WIN FOR FOREST

Cardiff Cup-holders beaten after scoring first

LET 'EM ALL COME, AND GO

" Well, if here isn't another of those Welsh chaps ! "

(It was curious that following on last week's Cardiff City visitation, Forest entertained another team from the land of the leek in Swansea to-day.)

Forest on the attack against Hull City at The City Ground in on December 22nd 1928. The Reds won 3-1 and finished 11th in the Second Division.

[left] A cartoon of Sid Gibson who appeared in 276 games for Forest and scored 55 goals

[next page] The 1928-29 squad photo. Back row, left to right: all unknown. Middle row, left to right; Jack Baynes (manager), unknown, unknown, unknown, unknown, Alfred Harrison, Jack Belton, David Willis (trainer). Seated row, left to right; William Thompson, Sid Gibson, unknown, Noah Burton, Charles Jones. On floor, left to right; Bob Wallace, Harold Wadsworth.

FOREST EARN A REPLAY

Another recovery after being two goals in arrears

A SHOT GOES THROUGH FROM 40 YARDS

ON TOP GEAR

"NOTHING LIKE 'GETTING THERE' SOMEHOW!"
(To-day was Cup-tie day again in Nottingham, and after the Sunderland scenes you know what that means.)

During another average season in 1929-30, the highlight was again an FA Cup run. The Reds beat Rotherham and Fulham and then set a new City Ground attendance record in the fifth round replay with Sunderland. Over 39,000 paid to see the home side win 3-1. They then faced Sheffield Wednesday in the quarter-finals, and drew an even bigger crowd of 44,166 to The City Ground (see picture on next page). As the headline above explains, Forest went 2-0 down, including a shot from 40 yards before battling back for a 2-2 draw. High-flying Wednesday won the replay 3-0 and went on to win their second consecutive First Division championship.

The 1930s

WALLACE

Bob Wallace captained the Reds and eventually played 269 games for the club before retiring in 1930-31.

[below] Forest travelled to Holland in March 1931 where they played a Netherlands XI and won 3-1.

ROBERT S. WALLACE
NOTTS FOREST

Opstelling der elftallen Woensdag 4 Maart

De elftallen zullen er vanmiddag vermoedelijk als volgt uitzien:

NED. ELFTAL

v.d. Meulen
H.F.C.

v. Run
P.S.V.

v. Kol
Ajax

Paauwe Sr.
Feijenoord

Paauwe Jr.
Feijenoord

v. Heel
Feijenoord

v.d. Heyden
Wageningen

Volkers
Ajax

Lagendaal
Xerxes

Tap
A.D.O.

v. Nellen
D.H.C.

Simpson

Dickinson

Dent

Loftus

Pugh

Mc. Kinlay

Barrington

Smith.

Thompson.

Dexter

NOTTS FOREST

[above] The Forest forward line in the early 1930s included, left to right; John Scott, Robert Heslop, Johnny Dent, Joseph Loftus and Alfred Quantrill.

[left] Full-back Jim Barrington made his debut in 1929 and missed only one game over two seasons.

[below] An excerpt from a local directory shows the corner between the Trent End and East Stand.

Nottingham Forest Association Football team playing on their ground at Trent Bridge

Photograph by " Nottingham Guardian "

[102]

Guildhall,

Nottingham.

W. E. WILLIAMS,
PROFESSIONAL ASSOCIATE
CHARTERED SURVEYOR.

ESTATES SURVEYOR
AND
ESTATE AGENT.

TELEPHONE 41513.

IN ANY REPLY PLEASE QUOTE
W/F.

3rd. May 1933.

Dear Sir,

PAVILION ROAD LAND.

It was resolved by the Estates Committee yesterday that the vacant land formerly included in Messrs. Dawson's Lease containing an area of **1190** square yards should be let to your Club on a yearly tenancy with effect from the 24th. June 1933 at a rental after the rate of £10.0.0. per annum plus rates.

The terms of the Agreement will be similar to that under which the adjoining land is held by your Club.

Kindly let me know that you agree to this arrangement in order that the Form of Agreement may be prepared.

Yours faithfully,

Estates Surveyor.

G. Noel Watson Esq.,
    Secretary,
        Nottm. Forest Football Club,
            City Ground,
                Nottingham.

T. GRAHAM (NOTTS FOREST)

THOMAS GRAHAM *(Notts Forest)* is a versatile player who has figured as wing-half and centre-half as well as a back, and has been a member of the team since August 1927. He was born at Consett and the Forest secured his transfer from the Consett club. Few honours have gone to Second Division players in recent years, but in 1932 Graham was England's centre-half against Ireland, and at the same time he also represented the Football League. Graham, who relies on ball play and craft, has cultivated the old style of combining attack with defence, and for several years has been one of the stylists of the game.   (No. 15)

Forest squad for the 1936-37 season. Back row, left to right; unknown, Horace Smith, Arthur Dexter, Percy Ashton, John Munro, Oliver Bowden, unknown. Middle row, left to right; Tom Peacock, Billy McKinlay, Henry Race, Tommy Graham, Harold Wightman (manager), Alex Wood, Daniel Edgar, Dave Martin. Henry Smith, Albert Brown, Gibson McNaughton, William Simpson.

[opposite, top left] Forest drew 0-0 with Manchester United at The City Ground in the fourth round of the FA Cup in 1935. Fans taking advantage of this away trip offer were well rewarded in the replay as Forest won 3-0 at Old Trafford.

[opposite, top right] Tom Peacock was a goal scoring machine for Forest in the mid-1930s. He notched 11 in 17 games during 1933-34, 22 in 40 in 1934-35, 20 in 30 games in 1935-36 and three in seven during 1936-37 for a total of 56 in only 94 games. He is the only Forest player to score four times in four different competitive games.

[opposite, bottom] A graphical depiction of the 1935 cup run.

SEVEN GOALS AND A CLEAN SLATE

DENNISON (1), MASTERS (2), MAWSON (1), and RACE (3), have scored Forest's Cup-tie goals, and intend to get some more, while Ashton has yet to see one go past him in the series up to date.

The above picture shows, left to right, Bob Davies, Len Beaumont and Tommy Graham. Graham made 390 appearances for the Reds while Davies (55 games) and Beaumont's (35 games) best years were lost due to the Second World War. Below and on the following pages show Beaumont's playing contract for the 1938-39 season, the last full season before the war.

Dated 4th July 1938

THE

Nottingham Forest
Football Club

AND

Leonard Beaumont

AGREEMENT
FOR HIRE OF A PLAYER

An Agreement made the 4th

day of _July_ 19 _38_ between _George_
Noel Watson of _City Ground_
Nottingham in the COUNTY OF _Nottinghamshire_
the Secretary of and acting pursuant to Resolution and Authority for and on
behalf of the _Nottingham Forest_ FOOTBALL CLUB,
of _Nottingham_ (hereinafter referred to as the Club)
of the one part and _Leonard Beaumont_
of _87 A Francis Avenue, Southsea_
in the County of _Hampshire_ Professional Football Player
(hereinafter referred to as the Player) of the other part **Whereby** it is agreed
as follows :—

1. The Player hereby agrees to play in an efficient manner and to the best
of his ability for the Club.

2. The Player shall attend the Club's ground or any other place decided
upon by the Club for the purposes of or in connection with his training as a
Player pursuant to the instructions of the Secretary, Manager, or Trainer of the
Club, or of such other person, or persons, as the Club may appoint. [This
provision shall not apply if the Player is engaged by the Club at a weekly wage
of less than One Pound, or at a wage per match.]

3. The Player shall do everything necessary to get and keep himself in the
best possible condition so as to render the most efficient service to the Club, and
will carry out all the training and other instructions of the Club through its
representative officials.

4. The Player shall observe and be subject to all the Rules, Regulations,
and Bye-Laws of The Football Association, and any other Association, League,
or Combination of which the Club shall be a member. And this Agreement shall
be subject to any action which shall be taken by The Football Association under
their Rules for the suspension or termination of the Football Season, and if any
such suspension or termination shall be decided upon the payment of wages shall
likewise be suspended or terminated, as the case may be.

5. The Player shall not engage in any business or live in any place which
the Directors (or Committee) of the Club may deem unsuitable.

6. If the Player shall prove palpably inefficient, or shall be guilty of serious misconduct or breach of the disciplinary Rules of the Club, the Club may, on giving 14 days' notice to the said Player, or the Club may, on giving 28 days' notice to the said Player, on any reasonable grounds, terminate this Agreement and dispense with the services of the Player (without prejudice to the Club's right for transfer fees) in pursuance of the Rules of all such Associations, Leagues, and Combinations of which the Club may be a member. Such notice or notices shall be in writing, and shall specify the reason for the same being given, and shall also set forth the rights of appeal to which the Player is entitled under the Rules of The Football Association.

The Rights of Appeal are as follows :—

Any League or other Combination of Clubs may, subject to these Rules, make such regulations between their Clubs and Players as they may deem necessary. Where Leagues and Combinations are sanctioned direct by this Association an Appeals Committee shall be appointed by this Association. Where Leagues and Combinations are sanctioned by County Associations an Appeals Committee shall be appointed by the sanctioning County Associations. Where an agreement between a Club and a Player in any League or other Combination provides for the Club terminating by notice to the Player of the Agreement between the Club and Player on any reasonable ground the following practice shall prevail : A Player shall have the right to appeal to the Management Committee of his League or Combination and a further right of appeal to the Appeals Committee of that body. A Club on giving notice to a Player to terminate his Agreement must state in the notice the name and address of the Secretary of the League or Combination to which he may appeal, and must also at the same time give notice to the League or Combination of which the Club is a member. A copy of the notice sent to the Player must at the same time be forwarded to the Secretary of this Association. The Player shall have the right of appeal to the League or Combination, but such appeal must be made within 7 days of the receipt of the Notice from the Club. The Notice terminating the Agreement must inform the Player the reasons or grounds for such Notice. The appeal shall be heard by the Management Committee within 10 days of the receipt of the Notice from the Player. If either party is dissatisfied with the decision, there shall be a right of further appeal to the Appeals Committee of the League or Combination, but such appeal must be made within 7 days of the receipt of the intimation of the decision of the Management Committee, and must be heard by the Appeals Committee within 10 days of the receipt of the Notice of Appeal. The League or Combination shall report to this Association when the matter is finally determined, and the Agreement and Registration shall be cancelled by this Association where necessary. Agreements between Clubs and Players shall contain a clause showing the provision made for dealing with such disputes and for the cancelling of the Agreements and Registrations by this Association. Clubs not belonging to any League or Combination before referred to may, upon obtaining the approval of this Association, make similar regulations. Such regulations to provide for a right of appeal by either party to the County Association, or to this Association.

7. This Agreement and the terms and conditions thereof shall be as to its suspension and termination subject to the Rules of The Football Association and to any action which may be taken by the Council of The Football Association or any deputed Committee, and in any proceedings by the Player against the Club it shall be a sufficient and complete defence and answer by and on the part of the Club that such suspension or termination hereof is due to the action of The Football Association, or any Sub-Committee thereof to whom the power may be delegated.

8. In consideration of the observance by the said player of the terms, provisions and conditions of this Agreement, the said _George Noel Watson_ on behalf of the Club hereby agrees that the said Club shall pay to the said Player the sum of £5=0=0 per week from _4th July 1938_ to _20th August 1938_ and £7=0=0 per week from _22nd August 1938_ to _6th May 1939_.

9. This Agreement (subject to the Rules of The Football Association) shall cease and determine on _6th May 1939_ unless the same shall have been previously determined in accordance with the provisions hereinbefore set forth.

Fill in any other provisions required.

To be paid £1 per week when playing in 1st Team Competition matches, also the usual playing bonuses allowed by Rule.

As Witness the hands of the said parties the day and year first aforesaid

Signed by the said _Leonard Beaumont_
.... and ....

George Noel Watson

In the presence of

(Signature) _N. Lightman_

(Occupation) _Manager_

(Address) _City Ground Nottingham_

Leonard Beaumont.
(Player).

George Noel Watson
Hon (Secretary).

BRAVO! MARTIN

Scores both Forest goals at Barnsley

STATUS SAVED IN LAST FIVE MINUTES

FIVE hundred Nottingham loyalists journeyed with Forest to Barnsley to-day to see the tug-of-war on the edge of the Second Division precipice. Forest needed one point for safety and Barnsley two. Dyson being still unfit, Burgin came in at inside-right. Barnsley's hopes that Everest, their right-back, would be available did not materialise, otherwise they were at full strength.

Barnsley. — Binns; Williams, Hinsley; Bokas, Harper, Logan; Bullock, Barlow, Hine, Asquith, and Bray.

Nottingham Forest. — Ashton; Trim, Munro; Davies, Graham, Baxter; Betts, Burgin, Martin, Surtees and Brown.

Referee: P. Snape, Swinton.

Forest hoped blue would be their lucky colour as it was at Villa Park, the change being necessary because Barnsley are also "Reds." A crowd of about 12,000 saw Harper win the toss and the Nottingham supporters hoped fervently that it was not an omen. Martin immediately sent the visitors away and Forest won a corner on the left when Hinsley kicked wildly behind. It yielded nothing, but Martin soon had Forest attacking again.

There rose a great Forest roar as the centre slipped a terrific ground-pass up the middle to Burgin, who shot on the run and saw the ball go inches wide of the post. It was all but a goal.

Fierce tackles, shoulder charges and kicking out showed the grim character of the game.

Martin was already a leading personality. In the Barnsley penalty area by sheer grit he wormed a way past four opponents to hook the ball just over the angle.

drew level rather surprisingly after 35 minutes.

ASQUITH, apparently beaten in a tackle 30 yards out, received the ball and shot first time, Ashton being surprised and diving a fraction too late to a swift ground shot which entered the bottom left-hand corner of the net.

A misunderstanding between Ashton and Munro almost let in Bullock, who nipped in with a header which the 'keeper only just managed to get round the post. Barnsley brought this half to a close with a storming rally and Ashton had plenty to do.   HALF-TIME:

NOTTINGHAM FOREST	......	1
BARNSLEY	....	1

Forest had the wind, but faced a brilliant sun in the second half, which started before about 15,000. Very soon Ashton had to punch away a corner kick, and when the ball was returned Graham kicked away close to the goal-line. Barnsley maintained a lively restart, and when another corner off Munro was awarded, Ashton caught the ball above his head from Barlow's head.

Forest were full of menace when they replied. A free-kick by Baxter was punched away, and when Betts headed over the goal-keeper, Williams, had retreated to cover the goal-line.

A tremendous backward leap by Binns saved the situation when a hook shot from Brown was speeding for the roof of the net. The keeper contrived to tip the ball over the bar before falling full length into the back of the net and entangling his feet in the netting.

Back raced Barnsley and Davies did well to block a shot by Hine, which went uncomfortably close.

Forest ended the 1930s battling to avoid relegation to the Third Division for the first time. In 1938 they needed some final day heroics to stay up. Dave Martin scored twice to earn a late draw at Barnsley. Forest survived while Barnsley were relegated. Both clubs had 36 points but Forest's goal average was just 0.002 better than the Yorkshire side.

[opposite] A year later it again went to the final game and again it was between the two teams concerned. This time they lost 1-0 at Norwich City but the East Anglians had required a 4-0 win to escape . Both finished on 31 points and Forest's goal average was this time better by 0.049.

Telephone No 8236.

Established 1865.

NOTTM. FOREST FOOTBALL CLUB.

ENGLISH CUP
WINNERS
1897-8.

Colours:
RED SHIRTS.
WHITE KNICKERS.

Members of
FOOTBALL ASSOCIATION, FOOTBALL LEAGUE, MIDLAND COUNTIES LEAGUE.

PRESIDENT	CHAIRMAN:	MANAGER	HON SECRETARY & TREASURER:
SIR ERNEST JARDINE, BART. J.P.	MR H. R. COBBIN	W. H. WALKER.	G. NOEL WATSON.

City Ground,
NOTTINGHAM.

Sept 9th. 19 39.

Dear Sir,

The undermentioned letter was placed on the Club's notice Board in the Dressing room this morning and I am requested by the Chairman to forward you a copy of same.
Sept 7th /39.

To the players.

The Committee much regret that owing to present conditions they are unable to carry on the Club in the normal way.

Players are therefore at liberty to seek other employment and the Committee hope all will be successful in quickly obtaining work.

When Football is permitted again – we shall immediately get in touch with you.

Signed H.R.COBBIN,
Chairman.

Yours faithfully,

S Mocclentone

Hon. Secretary.

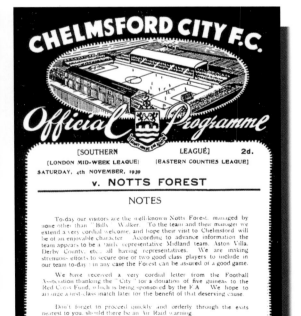

With the Leagues cancelled until further notice, various regional competitions were set up. Here are a selection of programmes from them.

[above] S. Flewitt in action against Notts County in January 1944. The two local rivals played each other 20 times during the six years of the Second World War.

[below] Programmes for the Forest v County game and a joint Notts / Forest side played the army in 1942.

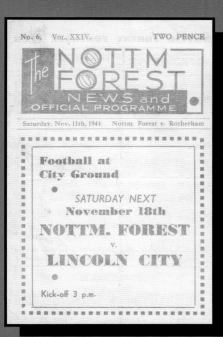

[above] Noel Watson served as club secretary from 1931 until 1960. He had previously gained a reputation as one of the finest referees around.

[below] Billy Walker, having saved Forest from relegation at the end of the 1930s, kept scouting for local players during the war. He ran a Forest Colts side of local youngsters and promoted many to the senior ranks after the war.

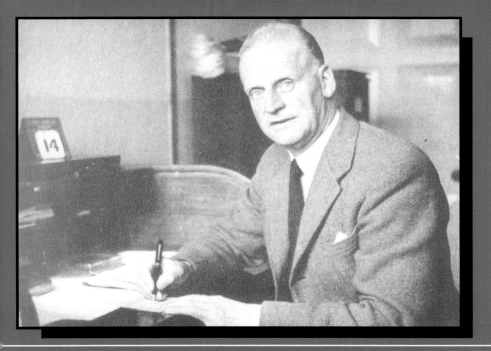

During the final season of war-time football, Forest played at Derby in January 1946 and then celebrated V.E. Day at the same venue four months later.

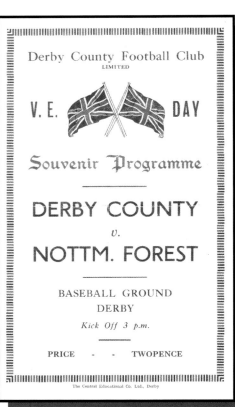

Derby County Football Club
LIMITED

V. E. DAY

Souvenir Programme

DERBY COUNTY
v.
NOTTM. FOREST

BASEBALL GROUND
DERBY

Kick Off 3 p.m.

PRICE   -   -   TWOPENCE

The Central Educational Co. Ltd., Derby

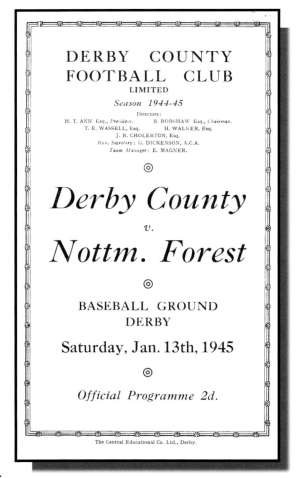

DERBY COUNTY
FOOTBALL CLUB
LIMITED

Season 1944-45

Directors:
H. T. ANN Esq., President.   B. ROBSHAW Esq., Chairman.
T. E. WASSELL, Esq.   H. WALKER, Esq.
J. R. CHOLERTON, Esq.
Hon. Secretary: G. DICKENSON, A.C.A.
Team Manager: E. MAGNER.

◎

Derby County
v.
Nottm. Forest

◎

BASEBALL GROUND
DERBY

Saturday, Jan. 13th, 1945

◎

Official Programme 2d.

The Central Educational Co. Ltd., Derby.

Heavy snows disrupted the 1946-47 season which dragged on into June.

[below] Left to right; Scottish international Frank O'Donnell signed for Forest soon after the war but played in only 11 games. Fred Scott couldn't stop Forest being relegated to the Third Division for the first time in 1949 but was an ever present in 1950-51 when they bounced back. In all he appeared in 322 games, scoring 46 times. After the war Forest adopted the 'Forester' logo for a while.

F. O'DONNELL

NOTTINGHAM FOREST

N.F.F.C.

COLOURS RED & WHITE

When the 1947 snows finally melted the rivers filed to capacity and then flooded. Forest suffered more than most and lost many historical documents stored at the ground.

[opposite] Forest captain Horace Gager.

The 1950s

The Nottinghamshire Guardian

WEEKLY

SATURDAY, DECEMBER 3, 1949.

No. 5,455.   12 pages.   Three Half-pence.

HOUSEHOLD LINENS

Stapleton's

FLOOR COVERING

CHEAPSIDE, NOTTINGHAM.

The ancient rivals meet again

NOTTS COUNTY

NOTTINGHAM FOREST

The players are: Nottingham Forest—(1) Bob McCall, (2) Harry Walker, (3) Geoff Thomas, (4) John Anderson, (5) Jack Burkitt, (6) Horace Gager, (7) Wally Ardron, (8) Fred Scott, (9) John Love, (10) Tom Capel, (11) Gordon Kaile.   Notts County—(1) Tommy Lawton, (2) Roy Smith, (3) Norman Rigby, (4) T. Deans, (5) Billy Baxter, (6) H. Adamson, (7) Jackie Sewell, (8) T. Johnston, (9) H. Chapman, (10) F. Broome, (11) W. Evans.

Also see pages 6 & 7

In 1949-50 Forest and County were battling head-to-head for promotion from the Third Division (South). Horace Gager and Tommy Lawton shake hands before the game. Notts eventual won promotion on goal average, while Forest (only two points behind) came fourth. Things were cordial off the pitch, on the left Bob McCall and Len Beaumont walk out to open the batting in a charity cricket game jointly hosted with Notts County.

A Forest line-up during a trip to Holland at the end of the 1949-50 season. Back row, left to right; Geoff Thomas, Bill Whare, Laurence Platts, Jack Hutchinson, Bill Morley. Front row, left to right; unknown, John Love, Fred Scott, Allan Ashman, Gordon Kaile, Tommy Capel.

[left] Colin Collindridge signed for the 1950-51 season and made an immediate impact as he played in all 48 games and scored 18 goals from the wing.

Tommy Graham (right) was one of Forest's longest serving members of staff. Here, snapped in 1948, he is blowing up footballs for training. He was the club's trainer from 1946 to 1960 having previously been a player from 1927 to 1940, playing 390 games.

Billy Walker addresses the players as they prepare for another attempt at escaping the Third Division in the 1950-51 season.

Forest battled Norwich City for the 1950-51 Third Division (South) championship all season long. They beat their rivals 4-2 at The City Ground. (Right) Wally Ardron scored the first goal and challenges the City 'keeper (below).

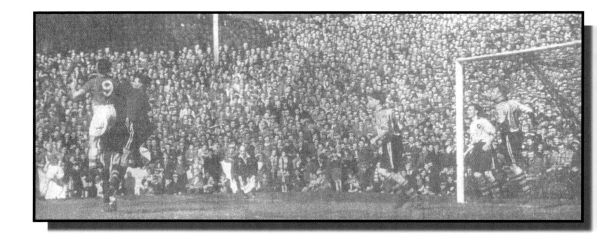

Forest need just one more point to be sure

TONIGHT THEY MAY BE CHAMPIONS

By A. J. Turner

Nottingham Forest 3 Southend United 0

IF Norwich City fail to win at Bristol tonight Nottingham Forest will be champions of Division III South.

Nottm. Forest's Brilliant Return to the Second Division

TWO CHAMPIONSHIPS IN ONE SEASON

Reds' Record-Breaking Experience

[above] The first team and reserves both won their respective championships in 1950-51. The reserves were in the midst of winning the Midland League for five years in row and they scored over 100 goals a season for 10 consecutive seasons!

[below left and overleaf] Forest clinched the 1950-51 championship by beating Newport 2-1 at The City Ground.

[below right] Action versus Port Vale.

Wally Ardron joined Forest in 1949 at the age of 30. He proceeded to score goals at an amazing pace and collected 124 in just 191 games, including the club's record single season haul of 36 League goals in 1950-51.

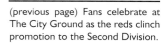

(previous page) Fans celebrate at The City Ground as the reds clinch promotion to the Second Division.

THIS AGREEMENT is made the _twentyninth_ day of _October_ One thousand nine hundred and fifty four B E T W E E N JOHN HENRY BRENTNALL of 18 Littlegreen Road Arnold in the County of Nottingham HAROLD ROBERT COBBIN of Houndsgate in the City of Nottingham Yarn Merchant FRANK FORMAN of West Bridgford in the County of Nottingham Builder GARNET SCOTTON OBSCROFT of Prior Road West Bridgford aforesaid JAMES HERBERT WILMER of 28 Austen Avenue Forest Fields in the said City of Nottingham Corporation Official HAROLD WRIGLEY ALLCOCK of 12 Stamford Road West Bridgford aforesaid Company Director JOHN GLENN of 80 Birlington Road Sherwood in the said City of Nottingham Company Director and GEORGE FRDERICK SISSONS of Fairhaven Cromford Road Langley in the County of Derby Builder and Contractor acting as the Committee of the Nottingham Forest Football Club and hereinafter referred to as "the Club" which expression shall include the Committee for the time being of the Nottingham Forest Football Club where the context so admits of the one part and JAMES SHIPSTONE & SONS LIMITED of Star Brewery New Basford in the City of Nottingham (hereinafter called "the Company") of the other part —————————————————————————————

W H E R E A S :-

1. UNDER and by virtue of a Lease dated the fifth day of December One thousand Nine hundred and forty seven and made between The Mayor Aldermen and Citizens of the City of Nottingham of the one part and the Club of the other part (hereinafter referred to as "The Lease") the Club are the Lessees of the Football Ground situate and known as the Nottingham Forest Football Ground Trent Bridge in the County of Nottingham (hereinafter referred to as "the Ground") for a period of twenty one years from the Twenty ninth day of September One thousand nine hundred and forty seven —————————————————

2. THE Club has agreed with the Company to permit the Company to provide erect and maintain during the period of this Agreement a Football Scoreboard on The Ground upon the terms and in manner hereinafter contained ——————————————————————————

N O W THIS DEED WITNESSETH as follows:-

1. THE Club will as from the date hereof until the twenty ninth day of September one thousand Nine hundred and sixty eight permit the Company to maintain a Scoreboard on The Ground such Scoreboard to be of such a design and erected in such a position as shall be agreed by and between the parties hereto ——————————————————————

The agreement for a new scoreboard in 1954.

Telephone No. 88236.

Established 1865.

NOTTM. FOREST FOOTBALL CLUB.

ENGLISH CUP WINNERS 1897-8.

Colours: RED SHIRTS, WHITE KNICKERS.

Committee:
G. S. OSCROFT, M.B.E. Chairman
H. W. ALCOCK, Vice-Chairman
F. FORMAN
J. H. WILLMER
J. GLENN
G. F. SISSON
H. LEVEY
G. SMALLEY

Hon. Treasurer: A. M. PARR

Medical Officer: DR. S. C. MATTOCK

Manager: W. H. WALKER
HOME PHONE RUDDINGTON 485

Secretary: G. NOEL WATSON, J.P.
HOME PHONE 85101

City Ground,
NOTTINGHAM.

May 10th 1957.

The Chairman and Committee of the Nottingham Forest Football Club desire to express their thanks and appreciation for the kind remarks and congratulatory message you sent on the occasion of the Club regaining its First Division status.

[above] Forest's reply to the many congratulatory messages they received after being promoted to the First Division in 1957 after a gap of 32 years.

[previous page] Forest players congratulate Tommy Wilson after scoring at Bramall Lane on April 7th 1957. The 4-0 win clinched promotion from the Second Division with Doug Lishman scoring a hat-trick.

The Football League, Ltd.

A. HARDAKER
(SECRETARY)

Telephone No.
4658/9 PRESTON

Telegrams:
LEAGUE, PRESTON

**6 STARKIE STREET
PRESTON**

19th August, 1957.

AH/T/D

The Secretary,
Nottingham Forest F. C.

Dear Mr. Watson,

At the last meeting of the
Management Committee, Share No. 35
in the name of J. H. Brentnall was
cancelled and reissued to Mr. H. W.
Alcock. I accordingly enclose Share
Certificate No. 146 in the name of
Mr. Alcock.

I must point out that Mr. Alcock
is the only person authorised to
represent your Club at any General
Meeting of the League. If, for any
reason, he cannot attend the meeting
he must appoint a proxy in accordance
with Articles of Association 40 and
41.

Yours sincerely,

Secretary.

League recognition of Harold Alcock taking over as club chairman in 1957.

No. of Certificate 146

FOOTBALL LEAGUE LIMITED

Incorporated under The Companies Acts, 1908 to 1917.

CAPITAL £5, divided into 100 Shares of One Shilling each.

This is to Certify *that* Harold Quigley Alcock *of* Nottingham *is the Registered Proprietor of* **One Fully Paid Share** *of* **One Shilling** *numbered* 35 *in the above-named Company, subject to the Memorandum and Articles of Association and the Rules and Regulations of the said Company.*

Given *under the Common Seal of the Company this* 19 *day of* August 1957

Harold Brentall

Directors.

Hardaker Secretary.

No Transfer of the above-mentioned Share will be registered without the production of this Certificate.

125

Forest's 1959 FA Cup run almost ended at the first hurdle. Drawn away to Tooting & Mitcham United, the Reds scraped a 2-2 draw then won 3-0 at home. Grimsby, Birmingham, Bolton and Aston Villa were all then dispatched on the road to Wembley.

NOTTINGHAM FOREST FOOTBALL CLUB

CITY GROUND, NOTTINGHAM

The Official Party will assemble at the

MIDLAND STATION

on Saturday, May 2nd and the train leaves at

8.15 a.m.

I would therefore be obliged if you will arrive at the Station at

7.50 a.m.

W. H. WALKER,

Manager

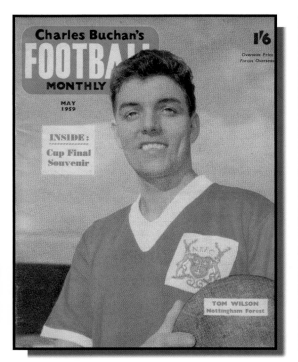

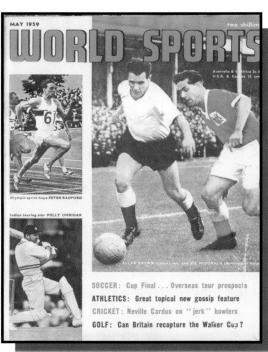

FOOTBALL POST

FOREST CUP FINAL SOUVENIR

Vol. L. No. 37. SATURDAY, MAY 2, 1959 THREEPENCE

FOREST WIN THE CUP!

TODAY'S TROPHY

Dwight & Wilson score

THE CUP OF 1898

AFTER 61 YEARS, FOREST HAVE AGAIN GOT THE FAMOUS CUP IN THEIR POSSESSION. AS EXPECTED, THEY WERE TOO SMART FOR THEIR LUTON OPPONENTS AND WON 2—1.

There was a crowd of 100,000, the receipts totalling £49,708. The teams were introduced to the Duke of Edinburgh and the Duke of Gloucester, President of the FA, Luton first, and when it came to the Reds' turn, the Duke of Edinburgh, after a chat with Jack Burkitt, spent a moment with Billy Whare, the second Channel Islander to play in a Final.

The present Cup was first played for in season 1910-11, Bradford City defeating Newcastle United 1-0 at Old Trafford after a goalless draw at the Crystal Palace.

SUN drenched Wembley provided a perfect setting for the Association Cup Final, 1959. Had the weather been ordered it could not have been better, and thrill seeking spectators were looking to the newcomers to the Empire Stadium, Nottingham Forest and Luton, not to disappoint them.

So far as the pre-match preliminaries were concerned everything went with well ordered smoothness for the Reds. The official party had a trouble-free trip to London, and after an early lunch quickly adjourned to the majestic twin turreted Stadium, reaching the scene of the game with over an hour to spare.

The Forest supporters in the crowd did their team proud. May be they were not able to match in head gear the Luton boaters, but they proudly vaunted their colours for the world to see and refused to be out-shouted by the exuberant demonstrations of the Luton contingent.

For a long time before the teams appeared the spectators revelled in the colourful pageantry and ceremony with out which the final occasion would not be complete.

The arrival of the Royal party brought a massed demonstration of affection from the excited crowd. Nottingham was honoured by the seating of their Lord Mayor and Lady Mayoress in the Royal Box, near the Queen.

A last minute rumour that Billy Gray had had to withdraw from the side was dispelled when the teams appeared side by side from the long tunnel, which leads to the dressing rooms.

Forest, in their neat white track suits, were led out by their veteran manager, Billy Walker.

Luton were in Cambridge blue track suits, and there was nothing to choose between the two in sartorial elegance.

and Burkitt brought a Continental touch to the scene by exchanging pennants.

Forest were the first to impress and almost immediately, Baynham was collecting a high centre from Dwight.

The Reds' football was beautifully ordered, and there was an anxious gasp from the Luton contingent when Groves slipped up and Quigley nearly wriggled through.

This was Forest in something like the mood we had hoped for but had hardly dared to expect. The first few minutes saw the Hatters entirely on the defensive.

REDS AT THEIR BEST

The first time they got away, Bingham was unable to control a pass from Brown and went for a goal kick.

The Forest supporters were jubilant, and not without reason. This was the Reds at their immaculate best, and nobody was really surprised when they went ahead in the eighth minute.

Imlach made a first-class run, and pulled the ball back to DWIGHT, who in his best manner, shot it into the net.

Poor Baynham. He could only stand and gasp at the velocity of the shot. So far there had been hardly a gasp from Luton. McKinlay and his merry men formed a solid defensive wall in front of Thomson.

It was not long before the Reds' supporters had something more to cheer—a second goal !

Again the movement was brilliantly conceived and executed. Gray wandered to the left, and WILSON eluded Owen to nod a perfect goal past the dejected Baynham.

TRAINER GRAHAM BUSY

Twice in the space of a minute Trainer Tommy Graham was called into action. First he had to attend to Wilson, who took a nasty body blow from a clearance. Next in the wars was McDonald, and in his case the Scot was led off after being hit in the face. Fortunately, he soon recovered, and came back to the cheers and the relief of the Forest following.

Luton tried hard to fight their way back into the game, and Thomson had a second attempt at a well flighted Bingham corner. The Luton defence was a bundle of nerves.

Wilson nearly snatched a third goal, the ball just grazing the upright; and then a swerving shot by Dwight had Baynham going the wrong way.

DWIGHT CARRIED OFF

It was heady stuff for the spectators and brought a constant roar of appreciation from the crowd.

Then, the Wembley hoodoo struck again—and Forest were the sufferers.

After an attack Dwight collapsed, writhing in agony. He had treatment from Trainer Tommy Graham, tried to rise, but fell

again. A stretcher was brought on, and the unlucky player was carried off.

It looked pretty ominous, and we got a nice pat from Brendan McNally as he was taken past the defender.

As was to be expected, Luton strove hard to cash in on the mishap to the unfortunate Dwight, but their work was not particularly tidy. Once, however, McKinlay daringly cleared over his own bar. It was an act of a man full of supreme confidence.

The Hatters were looking more together than they had done at any stage, but the Reds were far from outplayed. In one of their fighting thrusts, Baynham had a job to knock down an Imlach centre.

Had there been a full set of forwards, it was more than likely that before the goalkeeper had re-gained possession, the ball would have been in the net.

TWO AHEAD AT THE INTERVAL

Still, all credit to the gallant ten. They had played and fought like heroes, up to the interval, the score being 2-0 in their favour at the break.

The news that Dwight had sustained a suspected fracture of the right tibia stilled any fleeting hope of the ex-Fulham's man's return. What cruel luck!

Burkitt, too, looked as though he had taken a nasty one off the restart and lay like a log on the ground. Tommy Graham's magic sponge worked the trick, however, and it was not long before he was operating again.

This was indeed a pretty anxious time for the trainer.

Forest's policy was now more or less dictated by their numerical inferiority, but few gaps were left. Once however, Alan Brown found himself with a great chance, but his rising drive was smartly parried by Thomson.

Most of the play was in the Forest quarters, but the Reds were hanging on well, and the minutes were ticking away.

WHARE INJURED

There was no end to the Midlanders' woe and next Whare sank to the ground clutching his right knee. After treatment he limped back to duty.

It was agonizing for Forest. Seldom did they get out of their own half. At last, gallant and battered, they surrendered a goal and nobody could be blamed for it.

Hawkes moved upfield and his long cross found his way to PACEY who headed himself before sending the ball home and unerringly.

McKinlay was doing the work of two men as Luton, for the first time, showed that they could play football. Still they were fortunate to have this chance. But for the injury to Dwight, the final must almost certainly have been a turning one for the Reds. As it was they were clinging ever so grimly to their slender lead.

With just over a quarter of an hour to go the Luton trainer was called on to treat Brendan McNally who, after asking in vain, recovered quickly.

A flash of defiance followed from the Reds and Quigley burst through. His shot across goal was full of menace, and had Baynham worried before he saw it flash outside.

RESULT:

Nottm. Forest - 2

Luton Town - 1

Starlet Carol's international trial success

Nottingham's swimming starlet, Carol Hussey was second to V. Brown (Macclesfield) in the 100 yards backstroke event in the North v. South match at Bristol today.

She was 1.4 seconds behind the winner in 68.6 seconds. The match is an unofficial international trial.

Diane Wilkinson (Stockport) and Neil McKechnie (Wallasey), the Olympic and Empire Games free style experts, were surprisingly beaten in their individual events, but made amends by swimming well in the last legs of their respective relays to give the North an 81-75 victory.

This was the Cup won by Forest in April, 1898, and was the substitute for the one stolen from a Birmingham sports outfitters' shop the previous year.

DAVIS CUP WIN IN SIGHT FOR GREAT BRITAIN

Billy Knight and Bobby Wilson are expected to put Britain into the third round of the Davis Cup (European zone) by winning the doubles against Luxembourg in Mondorf-les-Bains, Luxembourg, today.

Britain lead 2-0 after the singles, in which Alan Mills crushed Joseph Offenheim 6-0, 6-0, 6-0 and Knight beat Franky Baden 6-1, 6-2, 2-6, 6-3.

Knight and Wilson face Baden and Gaston Wampach today.

Positions in other Davis Cup ties:
European Zone (first round).—Belgium 3, Holland 1; Spain 2, Finland 0; South Africa 4, Norway 0; The Lebanon 1, Colombia 3; Sweden 2, Hungary 0; Austria 1, Chile 3; New Zealand 3, Ireland 0; Brazil 2, West Germany 0.

Rough luck !

Surrounded by a sea of television sets assistants in a Nottingham store crowded round a battery radio set to hear a commentary of the match.

"We can't switch the sets on," explained one. "It's fire precautions, we must not have a crowd in here."

But quite large crowds gathered round the windows of television shops in the city where amiable managers had several sets going.

THE CUP GAME

"Got it again after waiting 61 years ! But it's a bigger Cup and it'll take more filling !"

NOTTINGHAM FOREST

(Red shirts, white shorts)

THOMSON

WHARE McDONALD

WHITEFOOT McKINLAY BURKITT

DWIGHT QUIGLEY WILSON GRAY IMLACH

Referee:
Mr. J. H. Clough (Bolton)

Linesmen:
Capt. C. H. Dennis (Army)
Mr. G. E. Readle (Manchester)

GREGORY CUMMINS MORTON BROWN BINGHAM

PACEY OWEN GROVES

HAWKES McNALLY

BAYNHAM

(White shirts, black shorts)

LUTON TOWN

[above] The Forest and Luton teams walk out at Wembley for the 1959 FA Cup Final.

[below] Tommy Wilson scores at Wembley to put the Reds 2-0 ahead.

REKORDS

Idrottsalbum

NOTTINGHAM FOREST

Nottingham Forest engelskt div. I-lag av
god klass. Har bl. a. vunnit engelska
cupen två gånger — 1897–98 och
1958–59.

Nr 10   1960

NOTTINGHAM FOREST

Bakre raden fr. v.: Jeff Whitefoot, Bill Whare, Bobby McKinlay, Chick Thomson, Roy Dwight, Joe McDonald.
Främre raden fr. v.: Billy Walker (manager), Tommy Wilson, John Quigley, Jack Burkitt, Billy Gray, Stewart Imlach,
Tommy Graham (tränare).

The FA Cup win put Forest in
the limelight across Europe. This
collectable Swedish print
(above) and German trade card
(right) celebrated the occasion.

[opposite] Mementos from the
celebrations which followed the
Cup Final.

The Chairman and Committee of Nottingham Forest Football Club
request the pleasure of the company of

L. BEAUMONT.

at a Dinner at the Savoy Hotel, London
to celebrate their first appearance at Wembley in the Final match
for the Football Association Challenge Cup

on Saturday, May 2nd 1959 at 8 p.m.

City Ground
Nottingham

R.S.V.P. to W. H. Walker
not later than April 16th

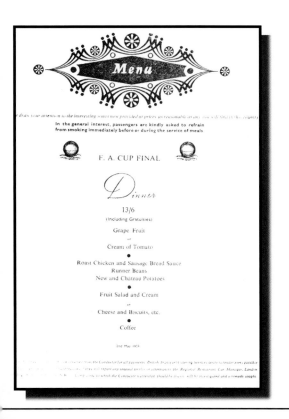

Menu

We draw your attention to the interesting wines now provided at prices as reasonable as any you will find in the country

In the general interest, passengers are kindly asked to refrain from smoking immediately before or during the service of meals

F. A. CUP FINAL

Dinner

13/6
(Including Gratuities)

Grape Fruit
or
Cream of Tomato
•
Roast Chicken and Sausage Bread Sauce
Runner Beans
New and Chateau Potatoes
•
Fruit Salad and Cream
or
Cheese and Biscuits, etc.
•
Coffee

2nd May 1959

CITY OF NOTTINGHAM
AND COUNTY OF THE SAME CITY

Dinner
at the Council House
Nottingham on Friday 8th May
1959

TO MARK THE ACHIEVEMENT OF THE

NOTTINGHAM FOREST
FOOTBALL CLUB

IN WINNING THE

FOOTBALL ASSOCIATION
CHALLENGE CUP
SEASON 1958/59

THE RIGHT WORSHIPFUL THE LORD MAYOR OF NOTTINGHAM
(ALDERMAN J. LITTLEFAIR J.P.)

IN THE CHAIR

These are the only known colour photos of Forest's victory parade through Nottingham when they returned with the FA Cup.

[opposite] Crowds flocking across Trent Bridge to see the FA Cup winners in action.

FOOTBALL ASSOCIATION CHARITY SHIELD

MOLINEUX GROUNDS, WOLVERHAMPTON
(Covered Accommodation for 30,000)

SATURDAY, AUGUST 15th, 1959   Kick-off 3 p.m.

Shirts:
Gold
RIGHT

WOLVES

Knickers:
Black
LEFT

FINLAYSON

STUART   HARRIS

CLAMP   SHOWELL   FLOWERS

LILL   MASON   MURRAY   BROADBENT   DEELEY

Linesman—Yellow Flag
R. L. HAMBLIN
(Cheltenham)

Referee—
J. MITCHELL
(Prescot, Lancs.)

Linesman—Red Flag
G. R. LEWIS
(Malvern Link)

IMLACH   KELLY   WILSON   QUIGLEY   GRAY

BURKITT   McKINLAY   WHITEFOOT

McDONALD   WHARE

THOMSON

LEFT

Shirts:
Red

NOTTINGHAM FOREST

RIGHT

Knickers:
White

THE TEAMS ARE SUBJECT TO ALTERATION

One of the thrills of the new season is captured in this picture of Wolverhampton centre-forward Henderson (right) and Nottingham Forest centre-half McKinlay, in a duel for possession of the ball.

In those days the Charity Shield was played at the home of the League Champions, so Forest travelled to Molineux to face Wolverhampton Wanderers. The Cup Winners were beaten 3-1 by the League Champions.

Season 1959-60

NOTTINGHAM FOREST
FOOTBALL CLUB

CITY GROUND · NOTTINGHAM

Official Handbook 1s.0d.

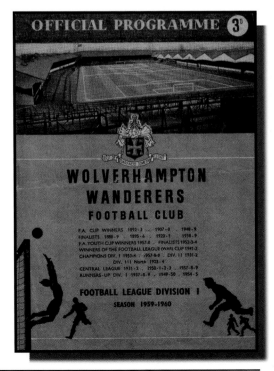

OFFICIAL PROGRAMME 3ᴰ

WOLVERHAMPTON WANDERERS FOOTBALL CLUB

F.A. CUP WINNERS 1892-3 · 1907-8 · 1948-9
FINALISTS 1888-9 · 1895-6 · 1920-1 · 1938-9
F.A. YOUTH CUP WINNERS 1957-8 · FINALISTS 1952-3-4
WINNERS OF THE FOOTBALL LEAGUE (WAR) CUP 1941-2
CHAMPIONS DIV. I 1953-4 · 1957-8-9 · DIV. II 1931-2
DIV. III North 1923-4
CENTRAL LEAGUE 1931-2 · 1950-1-2-3 · 1957-8-9
RUNNERS-UP DIV. I 1937-8-9 · 1949-50 · 1954-5

FOOTBALL LEAGUE DIVISION I
SEASON 1959-1960

The 1960s

Saturday, 8th April, 1961   Kick-off 3 p.m.

Bristol City Reserves v.
Notts. Forest Reserves

LONDON COMBINATION—DIVISION 1

BRISTOL CITY

RIGHT   Colours : Red and White   LEFT

NICHOLSON
BURT—2   PALMER—3
PARR—4   LINTON—5   BURDEN—6
TAYLOR—7 CLARK—8 STACEY—9 WILLIAMS (Ad.)—10 PETERS—11

Referee :
J. G. LEWIS
Glamorgan

Linesmen :
Yellow Flag :
W. R. Croome
Monmouth
Red Flag :
W. J. Harris
Glamorgan

RICHARDSON—9
YOUNGER—11 JULIANS—10   ROACH—8 ROWLAND—7
WINFIELD—6   GILL—5   WHITEFOOT—4
GRANT—3   BAIRD—2
ARMSTRONG

LEFT   Colours : All White   RIGHT

NOTTINGHAM FOREST

Late Team changes will be announced on the loudspeaker prior to the K.O.

OFFICIAL PROGRAMME   1ᴰ

B. & W. GOULDING LTD.

(Left to right) Roy Patrick, Tony Barton and Roy Dwight limber-up for training in August 1960.

The Late Mr. W. H. Walker

AS CHAIRMAN I would like to say what a severe blow our club has suffered in the passing of Mr. W. H. Walker—'Billy' to us all—on Saturday last, 28th November.

Most of you know that Billy was connected with the club for over 25 years and in the game itself for over 40 years. His record as a player was outstanding and there's little doubt that he was one of the game's greatest players with his only professional club, Aston Villa; he captained that club for many years and also captained England.

But it was as Manager of Nottingham Forest that we knew and appreciated him best, particularly during the post-war years when, after an indifferent spell immediately after the war and relegation to the Third Division, there was to follow—although none of us realised it at that time—quite the most outstanding period of success in the club's history.

Our friend—and he was a true friend of us all—firmly believed that the future of this club would be always on a secure basis if we set out to play good clean football at all times with the emphasis on team-work rather than the individual player.

We, of the Committee, shared with him the triumphs of promotion from two Divisions, of our Cup-winning feat and our firm establishment as a First Division force and his pride that our reputation for being one of the country's leading and most sportsmanlike teams was an accepted fact.

On his retirement in 1960 he joined our Committee and here his experience and wisdom of football matters were most invaluable and we, together with his managerial successors, Mr. Andy Beattie and Mr. John Carey, were able to call upon him for his opinion which he always willingly gave.

Billy is now no longer with us—and we all, Committee, Players, Staff and Supporters express our deepest sympathy to Mrs. Walker and family at this time—but he would have wished for no better epitaph to his outstanding soccer career than a continuance of our current performances and success.

We shall greatly miss him but it can truthfully be said that his name will always be linked with that of our club for he played a vital part in the shaping of our destiny and he would have wished no more for himself than that.

G. F. SISSON,

Chairman.

(following page) The Forest team as depicted on a Typhoo Tea collectable card. Back row, left to right; Joe Wilson, Jeff Whitefoot, Bob McKinlay, Peter Grummitt, John Winfield, Dennis Mochan. Front row, left to right; Trevor Hockey, Colin Addison, Frank Wignall, John Quigley, Richard Le Flem.

Forest players seem to be in good spirits as they take a training run over the old Colwick level crossing.

[left] Programmes from the 1963 and 1964 County Cup competitions.

[right] Bob McKinlay became 'Mr. Nottingham Forest' during the 1960s. He made his debut back in 1951 and over 18 seasons clocked up 682 appearances in all competitive games, still a club record and one not likely to be broken in the foreseeable future. Ian Bowyer, second on the list, is 141 games behind.

AMERICAN LEAGUE SOCCER NEWS

Vol. 31 No. 8   **APRIL 25 and MAY 2, 1965**   **No Charge**

Nottingham Forest History Colorful

Nottingham Forest's history is a colorful one, with many firsts, which has been accumulated over 100 years.

They were founded in 1865, which makes them the third oldest soccer club in England (only Notts County and Stoke City are older).

Among the club records are the following:

1874 — Shinguards were used for the first time in soccer when a pair were designed and worn by Samuel Weller Widdowson, a Nottingham Forest player at that time.

1878 — The referees' whistle was used for the *first* time in a soccer match in a game between Forest and Sheffield Norfolk.

1885 — Nottingham Forest played against Scottish Club Queen's Park in a F.A. Cup semifinal at the Merchiston Castle Ground in Edinburgh. This was the *first* and only occasion that a semifinal tie of the FA Cup has been played in Scotland.

1889 — Played against Linfield, the Irish Club, in a F.A. Cup match, and so became the *only* club in the history of the competition to have met opposition from Ireland, Scotland and Wales.

1891 — Renounced amateur status and became a professional club.

1891 — Crossbars and goalnets (instead of merely having rope stretched across two uprights) appeared for the *first* time in soccer when in a match between the North and South they were used at Nottingham Forest's ground.

1891 — Frank and Fred Forman, brothers who played for Nottingham Forest, also played international games against Ireland, Scotland and Wales, a feat without parallel in English soccer.

ASL Awards Ballots Mailed.

Ballots for the American Soccer League Manager of the Year and the Most Valuable Player Awards for the 1964-1965 season are in the mail. When received the results will be tabulated and announcement will be made at an early date.

Hartford, Philadelphia, New York Host

Nottingham Forest's Stars To Play a 10-Game Schedule

Since the announcement by the American Soccer League that Nottingham Forest would tour the United States and Canada under their sponsorship, many eyes have been turned in the direction of England where the leaders are engaged in a titanic struggle for First Division honors.

Nottingham Forest, too, are in the thick of the pennant drive.

Meantime, ASL officials have not been idle in arranging a schedule for Forest's star-studded team.

A 10-game tour will see the English booters playing on the Atlantic and Pacific seaboards.

Nottingham Forest opens its schedule May 14 in a night game at Dillon Stadium, Hartford, against the Hartford all-star team of the ASL, with the next game carded for May 16 against the Ukrainian Nationals in Philadelphia.

The third game pits the English team against Hannover '96 of West Germany on May 23 at Randalls Island Stadium, New York City.

The itinerary:

May 14, Dillon Stadium, Hartford. vs. Hartford All-Stars.
May 16, Houston Field, Philadelphia.
    vs. Ukrainian Nationals.
May 23, Randalls Island Stadium, New York.
    vs. Hannover '96, of West Germany.
May 26, St. Louis. vs. Catholic Youth All-Stars.
May 30, Soldiers Field, Chicago. vs. Hannover '96.
June 2, Candlestick Park, San Francisco. vs. Hannover '96.
June 6, Coliseum, Los Angeles. vs. Hannover '96.
June 9, Vancouver. vs. British Columbia All-Stars.
June 12, Empire Stadium, Vancouver.
    vs. Hibernians, of Scotland.
June 14, Varsity Stadium, Toronto. vs. Toronto All-Stars.

A Durable Scot.

Bob McKinley is a durable Scotsman who on March 13, 1965, played his 273rd game in a row for Nottingham Forest — more than five years of perfect attendance. Incidentally, it also marked McKinley's 500th appearance for Forest. He is a center-halfback.

Nottingham Forest Has Quality - - And Winning Stamina

Writing in England's "Soccer Star," dated Sept. 18, 1964, Leslie Page made pertinent observations relative to Nottingham Forest. These were made long before the English club would tour the United States and Canada.

"Manager Johnny Carey, who not so long ago carried Leyton Orient into (English) Division 1, has assembled at Nottingham's City Ground an amazing amount of talent, some of which did not fit in elsewhere.

"Carey paid good fees for these players and also made shrewd exchanges.

"John Barnwell, always worth a great deal more than Arsenal gave him credit for, is at inside forward. Then there are Alan Hinton and Chris Crowe, both ex-Wolverhampton Wanderers stars. Hinton, shooting from the wing on the run and his movements from the touchline is still as good as anything in the League. Supported in the front line by Frank Wignall, former Everton player and Colin Addison, Nottingham Forest has one of the foremost attacking front lines in the English First Division.

"They fell down last year, primarily in home games. Away from home, they lost only four more matches than Liverpool, the champions. There is obviously quality and winning stamina in this Nottingham Forest eleven, and they could be a strange outside bet for National honors."

Only 300 Yards Separate Rivals.

The grounds of Notts Forest (founded in 1863 and the oldest League club in the world) and Nottingham Forest, two years younger, who celebrate 100 years of existence this year, are only 300 yards apart. Their stadiums are situated on either side of the River Trent.

AMERICAN LEAGUE SOCCER NEWS
Published by American Soccer League, Inc.
Affiliated with the U. S. Soccer Football Assn.
KURT LAMM, *President*
JULIUS ALONSO, *Secy.*, 772 East 37th St., Brooklyn 10, N. Y.
News items for American Soccer League News should be sent to EDITOR ERIC CHARLESON, 2134 Glebe Avenue, New York 62, N. Y.

Four Managers in 100 Years.

Nottingham Forest has had only four managers in its long and colorful history. Under one of them, W. H. (Billy) Walker, who until he retired in 1960, had been the Forest's pilot for 21 years. Whilst manager, Walker guided the red-shirts to an English Football Assn. Cup final win in 1959, beating Luton Town, 2-1, at Wembley Stadium to become the first team ever to win the cup with only 10 men. Roy Dwight, outside right, suffered a broken leg midway through the first period after scoring Forest's second goal.

Nottingham Forest In Europe.

Although a tour of Spain was cancelled in the spring of 1964, nevertheless the Foresters made their presence felt when they toured Germany and Switzerland instead.

Playing against Hertha BSC in Berlin, the English booters shut out the German team by a 3-0 score. Traveling on for more honors, Nottingham next played three games in Switzerland, winning 6-0 against Basle, winning again against Lucerne, 4-0, with a windup against Winterthur, this time by a 5-1 score. Totals, in four games, 18 goals scored against the opposition with only one against. That's soccer, brother! 'Nuff said!

Just a Reminder.

There will be a 15-minute intermission between halves of American Soccer League and Eastern Soccer Conference games this season.

AMERICAN SOCCER LEAGUE STANDINGS
(As of April 19th, 1965)

	P	W	T	L	Pts	Goals F	A
Hartford	9	8	0	1	16	22	9
Newark Portuguese	9	6	0	3	12	20	10
Roma	10	5	2	3	12	21	18
N.B. Hungarian	8	3	1	4	7	24	23
Uhrik Truckers	8	2	1	5	5	9	18
Falcons	8	0	0	8	0	8	26

SCHEDULE

April 25th
FALCONS vs. UHRIK TRUCKERS AT IRONBOUND FIELD, NEWARK, N.J.—2:30 P.M.

May 2nd
NEWARK PORTUGUESE vs. HARTFORD AT IRONBOUND FIELD, NEWARK, N.J.—2:30 P.M.

May 9th
FALCONS vs. N.B. HUNGARIAN AT IRONBOUND FIELD, NEWARK, N.J.—2:30 P.M.

May 16th
UHRIK TRUCKERS vs. N.B. HUNGARIAN AT PHILADELPHIA, PA.—2:30 P.M.

RESULTS

April 11th
HARTFORD 3   N.B. HUNGARIAN 2
Hartford—Domico Giovmantino 48 mins, John Kerr 60 and 67 mins.
N.B.—Roland Rackauskas 6 mins, Wm. Drake 70 mins.

ASL TOP GOALSCORERS

Herculiana Figuerdo 7	Americo Sadiotte, Roma 4
Otto Weber, N.B. Hungarians 5	Julius Roth, N.B. Hungarian 4
Michael Wieszt, N.B. Hungarian 5	Tommy McLeod, Hartford 4

EASTERN CONFERENCE STANDINGS
(As of April 19th, 1965)
NORTH DIVISION

	P	W	T	L	Pts	Goals F	A
BW Gottschee	15	9	1	5	19	26	20
German-Hungarian	13	7	2	4	16	34	27
Giuliana	12	5	5	2	15	26	17
Boston Metros	11	4	3	4	11	21	20
N. Y. Hungaria	11	4	3	4	11	22	21
Newark Ukrainian	13	1	1	10	4	12	37

SOUTH DIVISION

	P	W	T	L	Pts	Goals F	A
N. Y. Ukrainian	14	8	3	3	19	32	12
Ukrainian Nationals	14	7	5	2	19	30	14
N. Y. Inter	13	5	5	3	15	24	24
N. Y. Hota	13	5	4	4	14	17	14
N. Y. American	14	3	4	7	10	18	31
Greek-American	9	3	2	4	8	15	21
Minerva-Pfaelzer	14	2	1	11	5	11	30

SCHEDULE

April 25th, 1965
NATIONAL CHALLENGE CUP
GERMAN-HUNGARIAN vs. N. Y. UKRAINIAN AT METROPOLITAN OVAL, MASPETH—2:30 P.M.
UKRAINIAN NATIONALS vs. BOSTON AT PHILADELPHIA, PA.—2:30 P.M.

CONFERENCE
N. Y. AMERICAN vs. NEWARK UKRAINIAN AT UKRAINIAN FIELD, COLLEGE POINT—2 P.M.
N. Y. INTER vs. MINERVA-PFAELZER AT UKRAINIAN FIELD, COLLEGE POINT—2:30 P.M.
HOTA vs. GIULIANA AT EINTRACHT OVAL, ASTORIA—2:30 P.M.
N. Y. HUNGARIA vs. GREEK-AMERICAN AT SCHUETZEN PARK, NO. BERGEN, N.J.—2:30 P.M.

RESULTS

April 11th
NATIONAL CHALLENGE CUP — N. Y. Semi-Final
N. Y. UKRAINIAN 1   GIULIANA 0

CONFERENCE
N. Y. HOTA 2   BW GOTTSCHEE 1
GERMAN-HUNGARIAN 3   N. Y. AMERICAN 1
NEWARK UKRAINIAN 1   MINERVA-PFAELZER 2

EXHIBITION
UKRAINIAN NATIONALS 3   N. Y. INTER 0
BOSTON 2   GREEK-AMERICAN 0

Forest's Centenary year saw several celebrations take place. These included the centenary match against Valencia, a presentation of red shirts from Arsenal in recognition of the ones that Forest gave them when they formed in 1886 and a dinner at the Council House.

[opposite] Joe Baker leaving training in the City Ground car park.

NOTTINGHAM FOREST			VALENCIA C. de F.
Red Shirts, White Shorts			White Shirts, White Shorts

NOTTINGHAM FOREST			VALENCIA C. de F.	
Peter GRUMMITT	1		1	Ricardo ZAMORA
Peter HINDLEY	2		2	Garcia VERDUGO
Denis MOCHAN	3		3	Francisco VIDAGANY
Henry NEWTON	4		4	Jose EGEA
Bobby McKINLAY	5		5	Manuel MESTRE
Jeffrey WHITEFOOT	6		6	ROBERTO Gil
Chris CROWE	7		7	Manuel POLI
Colin ADDISON	8		8	Jose Maria SANCHEZ LAGE
Frank WIGNALL	9		9	WALDO Machado
John BARNWELL	10		10	Vicente GUILLOT
Alan HINTON	11		11	Juan MUÑOZ

PRESENTATION

At 7.15 p.m. Mr. D. J. C. H. Hill-Wood, M.C., Chairman of Arsenal Football Club will present a Ceramic Gun to Mr. G. F. Sisson, Chairman of Nottingham Forest Football Club, as a memento of the occasion.

He will also present a set of jerseys, reciprocating a similar gift made by Forest to Arsenal when their club was founded.

7.25 p.m.
Spanish National Anthem.
British National Anthem.

Referee : Mr. W. Clements (West Bromwich)

Linesmen : Mr. S. B. Stoakes, Coun. D. C. Birkenshaw

Still rated as one of Forest's greatest ever games over 40 years later, the FA Cup quarter-final against Everton at The City Ground in 1967 was the highlight of a memorable season. As the season progressed, the Reds built up a furious pace and by April they were on a run of only one defeat in 28 League and Cup games. This run had given them a realistic chance of doing the double. Ian Storey-Moore and Joe Baker were the biggest attacking threats with Moore having 14 goals in 28 League and Cup games and Baker having 17 in 38 by the time of the Everton match. The day would turn out very differently for the two of them. Moore hit a stunning hat-trick in the 3-2 win while Baker sustained knee injuries that ended his season. With Baker out, the Reds slipped to second in the League behind Manchester United (a team they had beaten 4-1 earlier in the season) and lost the FA Cup semi-final to Tottenham Hotspur.

[opposite] John Barnwell shows off the latest formal-wear on Thurland Street in the city.

A WONDERFUL DAY FOR FANS

WELL, what a day it was for Forest supporters! And what a night it was as Nottingham took on the air of a carnival city as thousands of jubilant Reds' fans went on the town celebrating their side's brilliant 3-1 win over Matt Busby's boys.

There was very little else to celebrate about on the soccer scene however as Notts. County continued their slide, losing 4-2 to lowly York City. Derby County crashed 5-3 to Bolton Wanderers after drawing level at 2-2 at one stage and Mansfield Town were just beaten 2-1 by Shrewsbury Town. Over at Beeston, Notts. RFC turned on a power display to beat Birkenhead Park 20-8 in the first encounter between these two sides here for six years.

Over 50,000 saw match to remember

If you count the special guest tickets, the press and the on-duty policemen and ambulancemen, it is clear that more than 50,000 people packed into Nottingham Forest's ground to watch Saturday's classic and memorable match with Manchester United, reports **TONY PRITCHETT**.

The electronic crowd counter, installed in secretary Ken Smales's office clicked out the information that the official attendance was 49,946 — and that's 2,292 better than the previous record, set up in October, 1957, when Manchester United (who else?) were in the city for the opening of the club's new East Stand.

MANCHESTER UNITED FOOTBALL CLUB ● OFFICIAL PROGRAMME

No. 15

UNITED REVIEW

1966-67 SEASON

6d.

M.U.F.C. v NOTTINGHAM FOREST   SATURDAY, FEBRUARY 11th   KICK-OFF 3-0 p.m.

BURNLEY v. MANCHESTER UNITED, February 4th, 1967.
Despite Burnley defender Merrington's desperate dive the shot from David Sadler rips through Burnley's spreadeagled defence and into the net. The subsequent penalty—virtually on the final whistle—made the splendid game a one all draw.
Photograph by courtesy of Ormisher Sports Pictures, 109 Lord Street, Southport.

John Winfield challenges Harry Redknapp at Upton Park.

F.A. CUP SEMI-FINAL

KICK OFF 3·0 P.M.
SATURDAY 29TH APRIL 1967

NOTTINGHAM FOREST
VERSUS
TOTTENHAM HOTSPUR

OFFICIAL 1/- PROGRAMME

at Hillsborough

A great season ended in disappointment at Hillsborough. Frank Wignall fires over with this chance and Forest lost 2-1.

[next page] By the late 1960s Forest had a massive squad. Forty-one players were included on this team photo.

A SHATTERED DREAM

Gallant Forest come to end of Wembley trail against Spurs

FOREST'S dreams of Wembley and FA Cup glory were shattered at Hillsborough on Saturday when they went down 2-1 to Spurs in a thrilling match. But what a fight they made of it. Trailing 2-0 with less than ten minutes left, they staged a magnificent rally to reduce the arrears through Terry Hennessey and had another attempt kicked off the line. But the final whistle arrived with the Londoners, for whom Jimmy Greaves and Frank Saul scored the golden goals, still clinging to their lead and earning the right to meet Chelsea in the final. It was a sad day for local clubs on the League front. Notts., following their improved form against Stockport County in midweek, disappointed their fans by going down 3-1 at Bradford City. And at Gillingham, Mansfield's hopes of winning promotion to Division II virtually disappeared when they crashed 5-2. Notts. RFC won the Notts., Lincs. and Derby seven-a-side tournament at Beeston beating Henry Mellish OB 13-6 in the final.

VICTORY!—NOW FOR ZURICH

Forest crush West Germans in great Fairs Cup triumph

by TONY PRITCHETT

NOTTINGHAM FOREST ... 4   EINTRACHT FRANKFURT ... 0

NOTTINGHAM FOREST will become the first English club to win the Inter-Cities Fairs Cup. This was the bold and confident prediction of the Reds' chairman, Mr. Tony Wood, after he had watched his team outclass and overpower the West Germans, Eintracht Frankfurt, in the second leg of their first round match at the City Ground last night.

Forest slammed four goals, had three more disallowed, on a night when they never gave a disappointing German side the slightest hope of pulling back the two-goal lead established in Germany last month. So the City Ground club goes through to the second round with a convincing 5-0 aggregate—and it's the Swiss side, Zurich, next.

It was at a reception for the two teams and officials after the match that the Reds' chairman predicted Cup success for his team. He said: "Prediction is dangerous, but here goes. I said before we went to Germany that we should progress, and I now forecast that, having beaten Eintracht, we shall go on to win the beautiful trophy."

There was never much doubt, once the match had got under way, that Forest would dispose of the challenge from Eintracht. The German team were but a

Germany's World Cup goalkeeper, Hans Tilkowski, had a miserable night that might have been far the rest of his career.

He was painfully at fault with the first goal, badly beaten by a Lyons header which was deflected and stranded, punched away in no man's land, when the Reds' dangerous little right winger headed the fourth. With such a hapless figure between the posts, little wonder that the Germans, without much spirit in any event, had become demoralised and completely overwhelmed by the end.

It was Baker, the man the Trent End youngsters call "The King" duly rewarded his subjects with two goals in the first half, virtually to put an end to the tie. He nipped in to get the first after Tilkowski had failed to gather a fierce shot from Ian Moore and volleyed the second, again after the nimble Moore had done the build-up.

Ruthless

After this double blow, the rest was a formality. I expected more, much more, from Eintracht even though they were remarkably weakened for repair

Chapman and then to round off a good personal match. Lyons hammered the final nail on Eintracht's coffin.

Baker then had a hat-trick denied him by the intervention of a linesman who ruled out a hard-driven ground shot by right-wing winger to atone, a great header into the net...

Forest had a second season in the Fairs (UEFA) Cup after finishing runners-up in 1967. In the first round they defeated Eintract Frankfurt 1-0 and 4-0. This presentation flask was given to the referee and linesmen after the home leg.

NOTTINGHAM FOREST
FOOTBALL CLUB

N.F.F.C.

INTER-CITIES
FAIRS' CUP
COMPETITION

2nd Round, 1st Leg

The Inter-Cities
Fairs' Cup

NOTTINGHAM FOREST

versus

F.C. ZURICH

Tuesday, 31st October, 1967   Kick-off 7.30 p.m.

CITY GROUND
NOTTINGHAM

After winning three out of four European games the Reds were knocked out on away-goals in Zurich.

END OF EUROPEAN TRAIL

ZURICH WIN ON AWAY SCORE RULING

A GOAL 18 minutes from the end sent Forest toppling out of the Inter-Cities Fairs Cup against the part-timers of Zurich in Switzerland last night. Zurich won this second leg 1-0, but with away goals counting double, the Swiss got through to the next round as a result of their one goal at the City Ground a fortnight earlier.

Outside right Winiger scored the golden goal for Zurich in the 72nd minute, just at the time when Forest were looking too strong and too well organised for them. This goal levelled the scores at 2-2 and ended Forest's hopes.

So, with fireworks exploding over the stadium and Zurich players mobbed by their fans, came the end of the Reds' challenge in European soccer this season. But in the numbness of defeat, there was cause for some pride. They had battled against morale sapping injuries and against a team unrecognisable from the defensive slaves seen in Nottingham in the first leg.

But Forest lost this game, not in the Zurich stadium but at the City Ground where first they failed to gain a clear cut margin and then, on the morning before departure for the return match, Barry Lyons and Ian Moore failed fitness tests and had to be left behind.

McKINLAY OFF

On top of this, John Barnwell, hit system poisoned by a heel infection was doubtful virtually until the last moment and played at only half fitness.

The final blow came when Bobby McKinlay had another episode in a growing chapter of misfortunes when he sustained a deep cut over his left eye which necessitated four stitches. He was off for 15 minutes and then played the rest of the match with a plaster over the wound.

Bearing all this in mind, Forest rewarded their supporters from Nottingham with some good football in a match which Zurich proved themselves ready, willing and extremely able to play attacking football.

Zurich attacked hard but without getting through Forest's back four while the Reds, with more limited attacks, had three or four clear efforts at goal only to be foiled again by that brilliant goalkeeper Karl Grob.

Grob saved well from Winfield and then superbly from Wignall and Baker but then was then lucky when a volley from Chapman

A Zurich attack on the Forest goal. Newton (No. 6 on left) watches as Hennessey, Grummitt (partly hidden) and Neumann go up for the ball.

TONY PRITCHETT REPORTS from ZURICH

Hennessey and Newton positioned themselves faultlessly and read the game cleverly. So the feeling grew that despite the speed of Kunzli and the wingers, Zurich had not the ability to score the goal they desperately wanted.

But in the 72nd minute they did it. Meyer, who had gone off in that clash of heads with McKinlay, had a centre headed out to the Forest left. Winiger, springing in from the opposite flank, got to the ball before the clearance could be completed and he first timed a low shot into the net.

It was a grievous blow to Forest for it was the only shot at goal that Zurich had managed since before the interval.

Yet it proved to be the nail in the coffin of Forest's Cup hopes. Martinelli was carried off soon afterwards and Grob made a last glorious save from the tiring Barnwell.

Then came the final whistle and little Zurich, thought to be comfortable opposition when the draw was made, had added Forest's scalp to that of Barcelona in the first round.

Zurich.—Grob, Muench, Kyburz; Leimgrubber, Neumann, Trivellin; Winiger, Martinelli, Kunzli, Kuhn, Meyer.

Forest.—Grummitt, Hindley, Winfield; Hennessey, McKinlay, Newton; Taylor, Barnwell, Baker, Wignall, Chapman.

Referee: F. Geluck, Belgium.

Only goal puts Reds out of Inter-Cities Fairs Cup

Bobby McKinlay—off for 15 minutes with eye injury.

A REAL COUGH DROP

MARTINS NO. 10 DROPS

Guardian Journal

J14453 G34,972   NOTTINGHAM, MONDAY, AUGUST 26, 1968   PRICE 4d.

MUSICAL INSTRUMENTS
of quality — at all prices
at
THE CENTRE FOR JAZZ RECORDS

Music Inn
22, Alfreton Road Nottingham

Forest cross the Trent

COUNTY TO RESCUE

Guardian Journal Reporters

MEADOW LANE is to be the temporary home of Nottingham Forest for their Division One and Cup matches. Forest may not be able to use their ground for the rest of the season.

Fourth Division Notts. County stepped in to offer their facilities to their cross-river neighbours after the disastrous Saturday fire that wrecked the main four-year-old £110,000 stand at the City Ground halfway through the match with League leaders Leeds United. The match will have to be replayed.

Forest chief Tony Wood gratefully accepted the County offer yesterday. The Football League promised the club as much help as they could give. Other clubs offered help.

United game off

The first Forest match at Meadow Lane — it holds 48,000 people, slightly fewer than the City Ground — will be against West Bromwich Albion in the Football League Cup Second round on Tuesday, September 3.

Forest's plight has been eased somewhat because this week's two matches are both away — against Newcastle on Wednesday and Everton on Saturday. But the glamour match against European Cup-holders Manchester United — last season it drew a record 49,946 gate — due for September 10 is off. It has been postponed to a later date.

Forest have applied for two Central League fixtures for the reserve team to be postponed.

Season ticket holders should . . .

Nottingham Forest supporters lend a hand in fighting the fire in the stand.

Firemen play a jet of water on to blazing television cameras.

Calling Arnold

THE ex-police inspector turned publican; the ex-licensee who is looking forward to a new life; the first boy to go down Gedling Colliery . . .

These are some of the characters introduced in Down Your Way in the GUARDIAN JOURNAL tomorrow when the . . .

'Come back' call to Czech President: 'Position worsening'

AS leaders of the Soviet Union's four Warsaw Pact allies arrived in Moscow last night for a summit meeting on the occupation of Czechoslovakia, the Czech Government was reported to have asked Presi . . .

Disaster struck The City Ground on August 24th 1968 when a fire ripped through the Main Stand. Luckily no one was seriously injured but the game against Leeds United was abandoned part-way through. Forest had to play their next six games at Meadow Lane.

[opposite] The mercurial Jim Baxter signed for Forest in January 1969, though he appeared just 49 times after his £100,000 transfer.

Season 1968-69

FOREST REVIEW

Football League—Division One

Volume 4 Number 12

1/-

NOTTINGHAM FOREST v SUNDERLAND

SATURDAY 14th DECEMBER kick-off - 3 p.m.

CITY GROUND TRENT BRIDGE NOTTINGHAM

THE OFFICIAL PROGRAMME OF NOTTINGHAM FOREST FOOTBALL CLUB

Season 1968-69

FOREST REVIEW

Football League—Division One

Volume 4 Number 10

1/-

NOTTINGHAM FOREST FOOTBALL CLUB

Welcome back to City Ground

NOTTINGHAM FOREST v ARSENAL

SATURDAY 16th NOVEMBER kick-off - 3 p.m.

CITY GROUND TRENT BRIDGE NOTTINGHAM

THE OFFICIAL PROGRAMME OF NOTTINGHAM FOREST FOOTBALL CLUB

Season 1968-69

FOREST REVIEW

Football League—Division One

Volume 4 Number 12

1/-

NOTTINGHAM FOREST v SUNDERLAND

SATURDAY 14th DECEMBER kick-off - 3 p.m.

CITY GROUND TRENT BRIDGE NOTTINGHAM

THE OFFICIAL PROGRAMME OF NOTTINGHAM FOREST FOOTBALL CLUB

The 1970s

NOTTINGHAM FOREST

Peter Hindley
RIGHT BACK

NOTTINGHAM FOREST

Jim Barron
GOALKEEPER

NOTTINGHAM FOREST

John Winfield
LEFT BACK

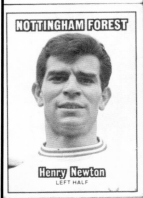

NOTTINGHAM FOREST

Henry Newton
LEFT HALF

NOTTINGHAM FOREST

Liam O'Kane
CENTRE HALF

NOTTINGHAM FOREST

Bob Chapman
FULL BACK

NOTTINGHAM FOREST

Peter Cormack
INSIDE FORWARD

NOTTINGHAM FOREST

Barry Lyons
INSIDE FORWARD

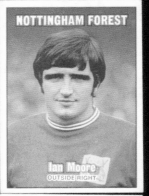

NOTTINGHAM FOREST

Ian Moore
OUTSIDE RIGHT

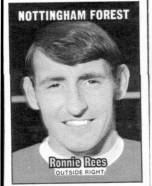

NOTTINGHAM FOREST

Ronnie Rees
OUTSIDE RIGHT

NOTTINGHAM FOREST

Alex Ingram
CENTRE FORWARD

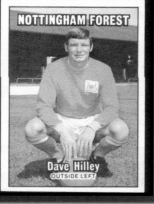

NOTTINGHAM FOREST

Dave Hilley
OUTSIDE LEFT

Forest players depicted on A&BC cards in 1970

A helpful photographer has pointed out Forest manager Matt Gillies in this picture. Gillies had taken Forest down to the Second Division in 1972.

Bob McKinlay returned to Forest as a coach in July 1971. Here he leads the likes of Dave Serella, Neil Martin, John Robertson and Doug Fraser on a run by the Trent.

Forest defend a corner at Stamford Bridge in 1971. Eric Hulme makes the catch while Liam O'Kane, Sammy Chapman and John Winfield look on.

TRAGIC END TO FOREST FIGHT

NOTTINGHAM FOREST 1   WOLVERHAMPTON WANDERERS . 3

WHAT a tragic end to Nottingham Forest's gallant but ill-fated bid to stay in Division 1. Despite producing some of their best attacking football of the season, the Reds suffered their heaviest home defeat in the final game at the City Ground last night to make relegation a near certainty, writes MIKE BEESLEY.

Dave Mackay welcomes new signing Ian Bowyer to The City Ground in November 1973. A few days later Bowyer found himself playing for a new manager when Mackay left and was replaced by Allan Brown.

[below] Frank Wignall (left) and Joe Baker (right) returned to The City Ground to play in John Winfield's testimonial game in May 1974.

REDS GO OUT AS THE MOB SHAMES TYNESIDE

Guilty glory for Newcastle

I LOST count of the number of people who sympathised with Nottingham Forest manager Allan Brown and his shell-shocked players as the bitter incredibility of Saturday's Cup exit defied objective reasoning, writes JOHN LAWSON.

The condolences will continue throughout this week as football fans everywhere deplore the manner in which the intimadatory Tyneside crowd dragged Newcastle back to a 4-3 victory in this infamous sixth round tie.

It was a sad day for me personally. As a youngster I stood many times behind the goal from which the rioting ins came to turn St. J....es's Park into an ugly, appalling battleground.

Police fought with the hooligan hundreds and as the teams fled to the safety of the dressing rooms, one of the Forest players was kicked and then punched in the face.

Fortunately, Forest supporters, so often criticised for their violent outbursts, did not accept the idiotic

never, even in such trying conditions, have allowed their position of overwhelming strength to deteriorate so alarmingly.

Manager Brown, outspoken in his condemnation of the Newcastle fans, acknowledged the point. "We were not professional enough when we went back on," he said as he accepted the most disappointing moment of his managerial career.

"We did so well after half-time but after the stoppage we failed to pick up our game where we had left off."

Captain Sammy Chapman, wearing the look of a man who had seen his soccer ambitions drain away amid the horror of that cha

[above] In controversial circumstances Forest were knocked out of the FA Cup in the 1974 quarter-finals by Newcastle United. Leading 3-1 at St. James' Park and playing against ten men the Reds looked certain to win before a crowd invasion by the home fans caused the game to be halted. When it re-started in a tense atmosphere United came back to win 4-3. The game was later decreed to be void and a replay was played at Goodison Park where the sides drew 0-0. The Reds had argued that the replay should have been at The City Ground so when the second one was also arranged for Goodison Park all three games had been played away from Nottingham. The Reds eventually lost the second replay 1-0.

[left] Northern Irish international Liam O'Kane made 220 appearances before his career was cut short by a knee injury. He then spent many years as part of the club's back-room staff.

[opposite] Allan Brown's tenure as manager was ended after a 2-0 home defeat to Notts County in December 1974.

FOREST NIGHT

at the

'HEART OF THE MIDLANDS'

on MONDAY, 21st OCTOBER, 1974

★ *We have booked this popular night club exclusively for Forest for the evening. This is your opportunity to enjoy an evening's entertainment with other Forest members and supporters, and any friends you care to bring.*

★ *The cabaret will have comedians LITTLE AND LARGE topping the bill — and there is also dancing, drinks and a meal if you want them. Allan Brown and some of the Forest players will be there. Why not make up a party of six or eight persons and book a table?*

Tickets cost 75p each (food and drink extra). They will be on sale at the City Ground today and before and after the Sunderland game on 28th September, and will also be obtainable, from 17th September, through the branches of the Forest Sportsmen's Club.

(Unfortunately the rules of the club do not permit people under 21 years of age to be present.)

HOOLEY'S GARAGE LIMITED. DERBY ROAD, NOTTINGHAM For guaranteed QUALITY USED CARS

EVENING POST

No. 30.024.   NOTTINGHAM, FRIDAY, JANUARY 3, 1975   PRICE 4p

CLOUGH TIPPED FOR TOP JOB

● RIGHT: ALLAN BROWN — deposed manager

● CENTRE: Brian Clough — tipped for the vacant position

● FAR RIGHT: Jim Willmer, the Forest chairman

FOREST SHOCK: BROWN IS OUT

[opposite] Brian Clough arrives for his first game as Forest manager in January 1975.

[left] Peter Taylor joined the managerial team at Forest in July 1976. Here he is seen shaking hands with chairman Brian Appleby while Stuart Dryden looks on.

The Forest squad that set out for promotion in the 1976-77 season. Back row, left to right; John Robertson, Paul Richardson, Martin O'Neill, Ian Bowyer. Middle row, left to right; Brian Clough (manager), Colin Barrett, Steve Wignall, John Middleton, Peter Wells, Barry Butlin, David Dall. Front row, left to right; Terry Curran, John McGovern, Sean Haslegrave, Sammy Chapman, John O'Hare, Frank Clark, Glyn Saunders.

RAMPANT REDS TAKE CUP IN STYLE

FOREST ... 4   ORIENT ... 0

(Forest won 5-1 on aggregate)

A STRANGER could have mistaken the scenes at the City Ground for those of promotion celebrations as Nottingham Forest completed their Anglo-Scottish journey in style last night.

Forest's first trophy under the Clough and Taylor partnership arrived in December 1976 in the unlikely form of the Anglo-Scottish Cup. The Reds beat West Bromwich Albion, Bristol City, Kilmarnock and Ayr United to reach the final where they overcame Orient 1-1 and 4-0.

KENNY BURNS

FRANK CLARK

JOHN O'HARE

PETER SHILTON
STOKE

Forest won promotion in 1977 and soon bolstered their squad for an assault on the top tier of English football. As can be seen from the football cards on this page, Peter Withe, Kenny Burns, John McGovern, Frank Clark, John O'Hare and Peter Shilton all came to Forest after Brian Clough became manager along with Larry Lloyd and Archie Gemmill.

PETER WITHE

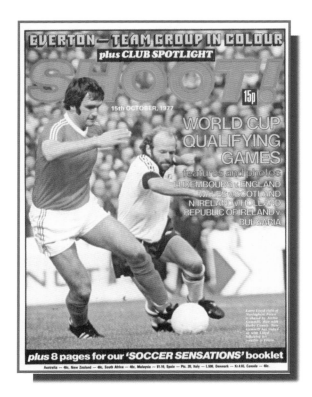

[left] This early-season magazine cover shows Archie Gemmill playing for Derby against Forest just weeks before signing for the Reds.

[below] Peter Withe goes close against Manchester City at The City Ground. The game was featured on Match of the Day as national press and media began to take Forest seriously. The Reds won 2-1 and topped the early season League table.

[above] As Forest topped the First Division table the sponsorship and advertising opportunities grew. Here the first team squad take delivery of a sponsored Toyota car.

[right] Viv Anderson came through the Forest youth system and flourished under the management of Clough and Taylor. He famously became the first black player to represent England and is arguably the best right back to play for Forest.

[above] Chris Woods (left) met up with Chic Thomson for this photo opportunity before the League Cup Final against Liverpool. Thomson had been the last Forest 'keeper to play at Wembley, 19 years earlier.

[below] Ian Bowyer battles through the Liverpool defence at Wembley in the League Cup Final. The game ended 0-0 and the replay took place at Old Trafford.

John McGovern was injured in the final at Wembley so Kenny Burns took the captaincy for the replay against Liverpool. The Reds won 1-0 and Burns became the first player of the Clough-era to lift a major trophy.

[right] Brian Clough and Peter Taylor in an informal moment.

[below] The team parade the season's haul of trophies before The City Ground crowd.

[previous pages] Forest were unlucky enough to be drawn against two-time defending European Champions Liverpool in the first round of the European Cup. A virtually unknown striker, Garry Birtles gave Forest a 1-0 first-leg lead and then Colin Barrett scored again in the dying moments. This photograph shows the players celebrating Barrett's goal as The City Ground erupts.

Forest beat AEK Athens 7-2 in the second round and then faced Grasshoppers Zurich in the quarter-finals. A flurry of late goals at The City Ground ensured that Forest progressed 5-2 on aggregate.

[opposite] Along with challenging for a second League Championship and enjoying a lengthy run in Europe, Forest won through to a second successive League Cup Final. They started slowly against Southampton but came from a goal down to win 3-2.

FOOTBALL POST

Vol. LXXI. No. 29   NOTTINGHAM, SATURDAY, MARCH 17, 1979   Price 8p

GARRY GIVES REDS THE CUP

DAVID STAPLETON at Wembley

TWO second half goals by Garry Birtles and one from Tony Woodcock, saw Nottingham Forest make history by retaining the League Cup here this afternoon.

Southampton had taken the lead in the first half with a goal from David Peach but in the second period it was all Forest.

In the best traditions of a Wembley final, sunshine bathed the crowds as they made their way to the stadium.

It all seemed a million miles away from Nottingham's weather, though fragments of snow had been swept beyond the touchlines of a pitch in good condition but liable to cut up somewhat.

Southampton's substitute, 19-year-old striker Tony Sealy, was a surprise. It had been confidently anticipated that versatile Manny Andruszewski would wear the No.12 shirt.

There was a bigger shock as Brian Clough relinquished the job of leading out Forest in favour of Peter Taylor. The teams were presented to the president of out Artemio Franchi.

FOREST	SOUTHAMPTON
Shilton	Gennoe
Barrett	Golac
Clark	Peach
McGovern	Williams
Lloyd	Nicholl
Needham	Waldron
O'Neill	Ball
Gemmill	Boyer
Birtles	Hayes
Woodcock	Holmes
Robertson	Curran
Sub: Bowyer	Sub: Sealy

Referee: P. G. Reeves, Leicester. Linesmen: J. Cross, Accrington; R. Bayley, Altrincham.

The Reds, winning the toss, elected to attack the tunnel end with their large army of supporters behind Shilton's goal.

Lloyd put a ball aimlessly out of play as he tried to find Woodcock down the left, and then Golac snuffed out Robertson after the winger had won the free-kick.

Former Red, Curran, made a menacing run in

FIND THE BALL – PAGE 15

Your TV matches

BBC
Chelsea v QPR
Bristol City v Middlesbro
ATV
Forest v Southampton

Southampton's first burst. He left Lloyd beaten for speed in an aggressive run but curved his centre harmlessly behind Shilton's goal.

The kick-out by the Forest 'keeper led to a threatening move, Birtles' head finding Woodcock who in turn fed Robertson. He skated on the outside of Golac and put an accurate cross into the middle where Birtles' header was easily covered by Gennoe.

The West Bridgford-born Boyer was wayward with an effort from outside the box as the Saints surged back.

But an incisive little touch by Boyer almost put Hayes into the clear, Clark showing his years of experience and reading the situation well to intercept.

STUNNED

Robertson again perked up the Forest fans by coming inside and forcing a save from Gennoe at the foot of the near post.

The Reds had settled rather the better and Barrett found Birtles with a chip into the goalmouth, but the Reds' striker was always straining for the ball and the header slid well wide.

Southampton were quickly back in the Forest area and Curran looked anguished as he went down, clearly believing he had received a push from Clark. But referee Reeves spotted no ill-intent and waved play on.

Forest were stunned by a 16th minute goal, stolen out of nothing by high-scoring Saints' left back PEACH.

Peach was at the hub of the move, finding Boyer on the left. He played the ball on to Ball whose chip through the middle was collected by Peach who went between Needham and Lloyd and slid the ball over the line with Shilton hesitating as though he expected an off-side decision.

Indeed, the referee looked long and hard at his linesman before giving the goal.

It was the boost that Southampton needed but they might immediately have gone further in front when Shilton had to plunge at the feet of Boyer following a Curran cross that had the Reds' defence in all sorts of bother.

There was no danger in Forest's response. Though Robertson again found time and space to cross into the box, the ball was always too high for O'Neill beyond the far post.

On the ball!

ENGLISH soccer went continental in the League Cup final at Wembley this afternoon in the shape of a new-look football!

The League chose their showpiece game between Forest and Southampton to launch a red and white ball which they plan to use next season.

Southampton were looking much the more incisive team now and Forest were fortunate that a Boyer shot struck Lloyd after Ball's centre from the left.

The goal had given Southampton tremendous confidence and they started to stroke their passes with complete authority.

One four-man move ended with Waldron getting his head to Curran's centre only for the ball to finish wide across his line.

Then Forest whipped up a more menacing attack and after Birtles, moving down the left, found Woodcock in the box, Gennoe had to be sharp off his line to save at the striker's feet.

O'Neill followed up with a poor cross that drifted behind after a rapid fire move involving Robertson and McGovern.

Ball was mildly reprimanded by the referee for bringing down Gemmill and Clark's free-kick found Gemmill with all the time he needed to pick out a colleague with his cross.

But it was a Southampton head that got the ball away.

LITTLE

The Reds so far had failed to strike a rhythm in midfield, with the result that the front men were being given little chance to show a cutting edge.

Although Southampton remained the more composed and Clark provided drama in their goalmouth as the half closed.

Robertson's free-kick was met by O'Neill, whose team mate Needham on the head and flew back to the midfield player.

He drove the ball back into a packed goalmouth and with the Saints defence still unable to get the ball clear, O'Neill got a third bite that was blocked.

HALF TIME:
FOREST 0
SOUTHAMPTON 1

Forest came out for the second half in the knowledge that they needed a vast improvement if they were to turn the game, not that Southampton was anything startling in a tepid first half.

And the Reds were desperately close to the equaliser in their first attack of the half. McGovern drove forward and sent Gemmill clear with a classic through-ball. The little midfield-man drove the ball against the out-rushing Gennoe when

Turn to Back Page.

DAVID PEACH (left) turns in triumph after beating Nottingham Forest goalkeeper Peter Shilton (on ground) to put Southampton ahead in the 16th minute

In the European Cup semi-finals Forest were drawn against West German champions 1.FC Koln. On a muddy pitch at The City Ground the Germans jumped into a 2-0 lead but the Reds battled back to go 3-2 ahead before being pegged back for a 3-3 draw. Ian Bowyer scored the only goal of the second-leg to put Forest into their first European final.

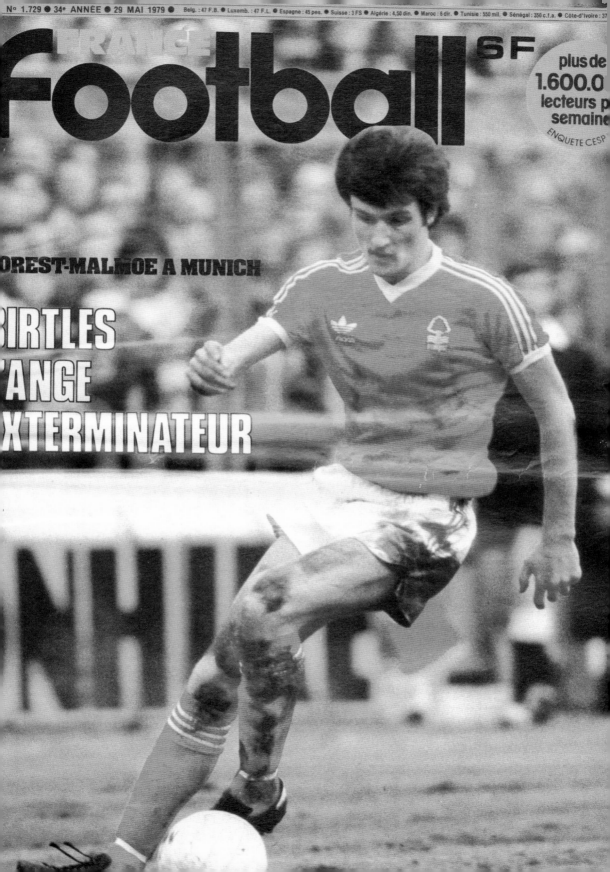

N° 1.729 ● 34e ANNÉE ● 29 MAI 1979 ● Belg. : 47 F.B. ● Luxemb. : 47 F.L. ● Espagne : 45 pes. ● Suisse : 3 FS ● Algérie : 4,50 din. ● Maroc : 6 dir. ● Tunisie : 550 mil. ● Sénégal : 350 c.f.a. ● Côte-d'Ivoire : 37

FRANCE Football

6 F

plus de
1.600.0
lecteurs p
semaine

ENQUÊTE CESP

FOREST-MALMOE A MUNICH

BIRTLES
L'ANGE
EXTERMINATEUR

...ttingham Forest gewann den Europacup der Landesmeister – 1:0 gegen Malmö

Oje — war das ein Trauerspiel

...rancis bester Spieler und ...chütze des einzigen Tores

Von Peter Kühn

...nchen — Der Europacup-Sieger der Landesmeister 1979 heißt ...ngham Forest. Vor 70 000 Zuschauern gewannen die Eng... er nach einem sehr schwachen Finale gestern abend im ...chner Olympiastadion 1:0 (1:0) gegen die schwedische Mann... t Malmö FF. Damit trat Nottingham die Nachfolge des FC ...pool an. Das Spiel im Olympiastadion hielt keinen Vergleich ...dem vor Dramatik knisternden Europacup-Finale der Pokal... r 14 Tagen aus, das der FC Barcelona in Basel 4:3 gegen ...una Düsseldorf gewann. Das war kein Fußballfest, sondern ...Trauerspiel. Jeder Nottingham-Spieler erhielt 10 000 Mark für ...Sieg über die harmlosen Schweden. Die Gesamteinnahme be... 3,5 Millionen Mark.

...ide Mannschaften began... ...iemlich matt. Oft tappten ...Stürmer in die Abseitsfalle ...Gegners. Und auch mit den ...binationen war wenig ...zu machen. Erstmals kam ...mung im Stadion auf, als ...ngham-Mittelstürmer ...y Birtles in der 8. Spielmi... ...seinem Bewacher enteilte. ...seite den Ball zwar über ...Möller, aber auch knapp ...s Malmö-Tor hinweg. ...ei Minuten später lud Lar... ...Lloyd den schwedischen ...außen Jan-Olof Kinnvall ...lich vom Torschuß ein. ...g unbedrängt köpfte ...dem Mann mit der Nr. 11 ...Ball im eigenen Strafraum

auch diese Gefahr an Nottingham vorüberging.

Sekunden vor dem Halbzeit- pfiff fiel dann das 1:0 für den englischen Meister. Nach einer Flanke von John Robertson köpfte Francis den Ball ins Malmö-Tor. Der für vier Mil- lionen Mark von Birmingham City verpflichtete Francis be- stritt gestern abend sein erstes Europacup-Spiel für Notting- ham.

Wer gehofft hatte, daß dieses Tor beide Mannschaften beflü- geln würde, sah sich getäuscht. Das Spiel wurde sogar noch langweiliger, die Zuschauer machten ihrem Unmut durch Pfiffe Luft. Es gab nur ein

... de der völlig überraschte ...vall konnte den Schnitzer ...ausnutzen und schob die ...kugel Peter Shilton in die ...t.

...Engländer hatten sich ...bald von diesem Schrek- ...erholt. Sie übernahmen ...utig das Kommando und ...en durch den raffinier- ...Birtles und den raffinier... ...Trevor Francis einige ...zen heraus. Ein Torerfolg ...e ihnen aber vorerst nicht ...t. John McGovern ver... ...e das Malmö-Tor knapp ...Schuß von Ian Bowyer ...e Möller ernst im Nach... ...en fassen. Die größte Tor... ...ck." Er strebte allein ... ...schwedischen Tor zu. ...legte er sich den Ball zu ...vor, so daß Möller klären

...f der Gegenseite unterlief ...n grober Fehler. Da... ...tte Kinnvall jedoch ein... ...sicht gerechnet, so daß

Mittelfeldgeplänkel zu sehen, beide Torhüter wurden selten beschäftigt. Die Schweden wa- ren viel zu harmlos, um die Engländer, die nach ihrem Führungstor etwas zurückge- steckt hatten, gefährden zu können. Raffte sich doch ein- mal Nottingham Forest zu ei- nem Angriff auf, so liefen die Stürmer meist ins Abseits. Und als Birtles in der 59. Minute frei vor Möller stand, jagte er den Ball in den Münchner Nachthimmel.

Alles klar hätte Robertson kurz danach machen können. Der alles überragende Francis war auf dem rechten Flügel unwiderstehlich davongezogen und hatte den Ball zur Mitte gepaßt. Aber der Nottingham- Linksaußen traf nur den Pfo- sten.

Die unbedarften Schweden wiederum rannten immer hilf- loser gegen die Nottingham- Abwehr an. Das Europacup- Finale wurde zum Trauerspiel.

...PROBLEM für Peter Shilton: Nottinghams Torhüter (links) ...ocht, nicht überlistet, als der junge Schwede Jan-Olof Kinnvall ...raschend zu einer Chance gekommen war.

DAS WAR DIE ENTSCHEIDUNG! Kurz vor dem Halbzeitpfiff erzielte Nottinghams bester Spieler Trevor Francis (links, fast verdeckt von Malmös Torwart Jan Möller) mit einem Kopfball das „goldene Tor".

Fotos: FMS

Nottingham – Malmö FF 1:0 (1:0)

● **Nottingham Forest:** Shilton; Anderson, Clarke, McGovern, Lloyd, Burns, Francis, Bowyer, Birtles, Woodcock, Robertson.

● **Malmö FF:** Möller; Roland An- dersson, Erlandsson, Jönsson, Magnus Andersson, Tapper, Ljung- berg, Prytz, Hansson, Cervin, Kindvall.

Auswechselspieler: Bei Malmö Malmberg für Tapper (34.); Tommy Andersson für Hansson (82.).

Tor: 1:0 Francis mit Kopfball nach einer Flanke von Robertson (45.).

Eckstöße: 8:3 für Nottingham.

Beste Spieler: Francis und Ro- bertson bei Nottingham; Cervin bei Malmö.

Schiedsrichter: Erich Linemayr (Österreich).

Zuschauer: 70 000.

„Unsere Stürmer waren zu dämlich"

Das sagte der Nottingham-Manager nach dem 1:0-Sieg

Von Berth Möller

München — Arrogant setzte sich Brian Clough, der Manager von Nottingham Forest, ans Mikrophon. Nach dem Gewinn des Europapokals begann er seine Pressekonferenz mit den Worten: „Der Europacup ist zwar ein schöner Sieg für uns. Unser Höhe- punkt ist er aber keineswegs. Die englische Meisterschaft schätzen wir da schon sehr viel höher ein."

Die Meinung seines Trainers Peter Taylor, der vor dem Spiel eine Menge Tore und einen hohen Sieg seiner Mannschaft vorausgesagt hatte, konnte Clough nicht teilen. „Ich habe gewußt, daß unsere Stürmer zu dämlich sind, Tore zu schießen. Und außerdem sind sie ja stän- dig in die Abseitsfalle der Mal- möer gelaufen."

Ein großes Lob zollte Clough

wenigstens seinem Vier-Millio- nen-Stürmer Trevor Francis: „Er ist ein ausgezeichneter Mann und hat sehr stark ge- spielt."

Ruhig und sachlich kommen- tierte Bob Houghton, der eng- lische Trainer von Malmö FF, die 0:1-Niederlage seiner Mann- schaft. „Wir hatten wenig Chan- cen, hier zu gewinnen. Es war schwierig, gegen Nottingham zu bestehen. Sie war

sehr stark. Besonders im Kopf- ballspiel. Wir haben versucht, über die vier Abwehrspieler mit langen, hohen Bällen zu operieren. Leider ist uns dies nicht gelungen. Nur wenn wir einen ausgezeichneten Tag er- wischt hätten, hätten wir die- ses Spiel zu unseren Gunsten entscheiden können."

Ein ideenloses Spiel atte- stierte Löwen-Trainer Eckhard Krautzun als neutraler Beob- achter: „Man hat deutlich ge- sehen, daß beide Mannschaften von englischen Coachs trainiert werden. In diesem Spiel war Härte Trumpf. Man hat viel zu wenig Ideen und überraschen- de Spielzüge gesehen. Dennoch geht der Sieg für Nottingham in Ordnung."

[opposite] Only Franz Beckenbauer had lifted the European Cup as captain more times than John McGovern. Here McGovern collects the massive trophy after the Reds 1-0 win over Malmo in Munich on May 30th 1979, just two years after getting promoted from the Second Division.

[above] How the German press reported on the final.

The 1980s

NOTTINGHAM F.

CITY GROUND

Chairman: S.M. Dryden JP
Manager: Brian Clough
Secretary: Ken Smales
Coach: Peter Taylor
Captain: John McGovern
Year formed: 1865
Ground capacity: 41,930
Record attendance: 49,945 v Manchester United, Division 1, October 1967
Honours: Division One Champions: 1977-78.
Division Two Champions: 1906-07, 1921-22.
Division Three (South) Champions: 1950-51.
FA Cup winners: 1898, 1959.
Football League Cup winners: 1978, 1979.
European Cup winners: 1979.
Colours: Red shirts, white shorts, red & white stockings.
Change colours: All yellow.

NOTTINGHAM FOREST

BRIAN CLOUGH
NOTTINGHAM FOREST Manager

A former England Under-23 and full international who was an accomplished goalscorer during his playing days with Middlesbrough and Sunderland. Started in management with Hartlepool but came to prominence with Derby. After short stays with Leeds and Brighton, he joined Forest in January 1975.

PETER SHILTON
NOTTINGHAM FOREST

Goalkeeper. Born Leicester. Ht.6.0.Wt.12.10. Age 29. Started as understudy to Gordon Banks at Leicester, and succeeded him at Stoke before joining Forest for £270,000 in September 1977. A former schools, youth, and Under-23 player for England with over 500 first team games, and didn't miss a League game in 1978-79. ●28(E).

VIV ANDERSON
NOTTINGHAM FOREST

Defender. Born Nottingham. Ht.5.11.Wt.10.4. Age 24. Started his apprenticeship with Forest in August 1972 and turned pro two years later. His League debut was against Sheffield Wednesday in September 1974, and now this former England Under-21 player has settled into the first team as a full-back. ●2(E).

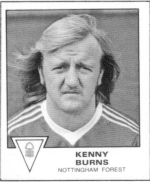

KENNY BURNS
NOTTINGHAM FOREST

Defender. Born Glasgow. Ht.5.10½.Wt.11.0. Age 28. Made his League debut as a striker for Birmingham against Hull City in September 1971, and transferred to Forest in August 1977 for £150,000. He converted to a central defender. Is a former Scottish youth and Under-23 player. ●14(S).

COLIN BARRETT
NOTTINGHAM FOREST

Defender. Born Stockport. Ht.5.11.Wt.11.7. Age 24. Started his career with Manchester City, where he made 53 League appearances before transferring to Forest in April 1976, after a period on loan with the club. Can play virtually anywhere in the defence, and in midfield too, if necessary.

LARRY LLOYD
NOTTINGHAM FOREST

Defender. Born Bristol. Ht.6.2.Wt.12.4. Age 31. Started his career with Bristol Rovers, but made his name during his time with Liverpool, where he made 150 League appearances. After a spell at Coventry he joined Forest in November 1976. A former England Under-23 player. ●3(E).

**DAVID
NEEDHAM**
NOTTINGHAM FOREST

Defender. Born Leicester. Ht.6.1.Wt.12.7. Age
31. Played over 400 League games during
a ten-year stretch at Notts County, and played
briefly for QPR before joining Forest in December 1977. Made his League debut in
1966 aged 17, and has won England B honours. Plays as a centre-half.

**FRANKIE
GRAY**
NOTTINGHAM FOREST

Defender. Born Glasgow. Ht.5.9.Wt.11.10. Age 27.
Started his career with Leeds, where he signed
pro forms in November 1971. Younger brother
of Eddie, he made his League debut against
Crystal Palace in April 1973, and clocked up
193 League appearances before his move to
Forest in the 1979 close season. ●7(S).

**JOHN
McGOVERN**
NOTTINGHAM FOREST

Midfield. Born Montrose. Ht.5.10.Wt.10.13. Age
27. Originally a striker, John had played for
manager Brian Clough at Hartlepool, Derby,
and Leeds before joining Forest. He is a
former Scottish schoolboy and Under-23 international and has over 400 League appearances in his career. Club captain.

**JOHN
ROBERTSON**
NOTTINGHAM FOREST

Midfield. Born Uddinston, Lanarks. Ht.5.8.
Wt.10.9. Age 25. This former Scottish schools
and youth international has now made over 200
League appearances for Forest since his League
debut against Blackpool in October 1970.
Has only missed one League game in the
last three seasons. ●4(S).

**IAN
BOWYER**
NOTTINGHAM FOREST

Midfield. Born Ellesmere Port. Ht.5.11.Wt.11.3.
Age 29. Started his career with Manchester
City, where he made his League debut in
March 1969, but transferred to Orient for
£25,000 in June 1971. Made the move to Forest
in October 1973 when Dave Mackay was in
charge. Gets on the scoresheet quite often.

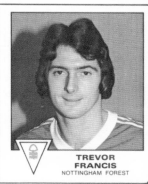

**TREVOR
FRANCIS**
NOTTINGHAM FOREST

Forward. Born Plymouth. Ht.5.10.Wt.11.7. Age 25.
A former England youth and Under-23 player
who hit the headlines by becoming Britain's
first million pound player, when he transferred
from first club Birmingham in February 1979.
Made his League debut aged 16 in September
1970, and turned pro in April 1971. ●15, ●2(E).

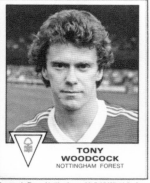

**TONY
WOODCOCK**
NOTTINGHAM FOREST

Forward. Born Nottingham. Ht.5.10.Wt.11.0. Age
24. A striker who signed pro forms for Forest
in January 1974, and after spending short spells
on loan at Lincoln and Doncaster, he settled
into the Forest first team. A former England
Under-21 player who has over 100 League
games with Forest. ●5(E).

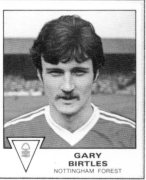

**GARY
BIRTLES**
NOTTINGHAM FOREST

Forward. Born Nottingham. Ht.5.11.Wt.10.12.
Age 20. Made his League debut against Hull
in March 1977, but did not establish himself
in the first team until 1978-79, when he made
35 League appearances and was the club's
leading scorer with 20 goals in League and
League Cup.

**MARTIN
O'NEILL**
NOTTINGHAM FOREST

Forward. Born Kilrea, N. Ireland. Ht.5.10.Wt.11.3.
Age 29. Started his soccer career with Distillery,
after studying law at Queen's University, Belfast.
He moved to Forest in 1971, making his League
debut against WBA in the November. Now
has over 200 League appearances and is a
regular choice for N. Ireland. ●30, ●4(NI).

[previous pages, 184-5] Paul Wilkinson begins to celebrate as his rocket shot finds the Arsenal net at Highbury during the FA Cup quarter-final of 1988.

[previous pages, 186-7] Panini stickers of Forest's 1979-80 squad.

It's time to renew your Season Ticket

ADMISSION CHARGES—1979/80

	Match	Season
GROUND (ADULT)	£1.50	£27
GROUND (JUVENILE)	—	£15
SENIOR CITIZEN	0.70	£15
MAIN STAND	£3.00	£60
MAIN STAND ENCLOSURE ...	£3.00	£60
EXECUTIVE STAND UPPER TIER	£3.00	£60
EXECUTIVE STAND LOWER TIER	£3.00	£60
MAIN CAR PARK	—	£10
MEMBERS	—	£150
CENTRAL LEAGUE—GROUND...	0.20	
SEATS ...	0.30	

Present East Stand seat holders will have first option on the seats in the Executive Stand and there will only be sufficient seats installed for the commencement of the season to supply these. A further announcement will be made regarding the price and sale of those seats which will not be available before the end of November.

SCHEDULE OF DATES FOR SALE OF SEATS

Main Stand and Enclosure — now renewing.
Block 'R' for Executive Stand — commence 14th May.
Blocks 'P', 'Q', 'S', and 'T' for Executive Stand — commence 21st May.
Transfers from Main Stand to Executive Stand — commence 1st June (limited number only can be accepted initially).
All options for retaining present seats expire 12 noon, 9th June.
Seat exchanges 11th to 13th June inclusive.
Ground season ticket holders wishing to purchase a seat—commence 18th June.
Open sales commence 25th June.
There will be no East Car Park Terrace tickets next season.
Terrace season tickets now renewing.

NOTE: The club will now be closed from Monday to Thursday, 28th to 31st May.

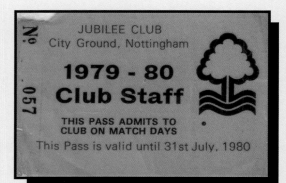

Nº 057

JUBILEE CLUB
City Ground, Nottingham

1979 - 80
Club Staff

THIS PASS ADMITS TO
CLUB ON MATCH DAYS

This Pass is valid until 31st July, 1980

MEMBERSHIP
CARD
1979-80

NAME ___ S. B. HODGE ___

No. ___ 17572 ___

CLUB ___ NOTTINGHAM FOREST F.C. ___

A sombre looking pair of Peter Taylor and Tony Woodcock as news breaks of Woodcock's transfer to 1.FC Koln in November 1979.

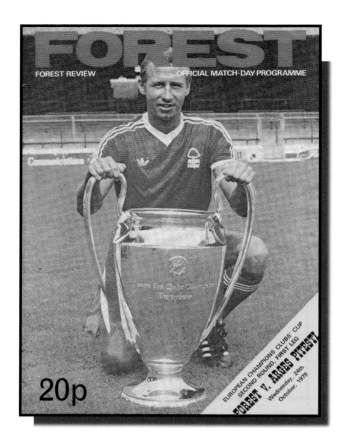

Forest began their defence of the European Cup with relatively straight-forward wins over Oesters Vaxjo (3-1) and Arges Pitesti (4-1).

[below] Forest won the BBC Team of the Year at the end of 1979

In search of an unprecedented third straight League Cup win, Forest faced Liverpool in the semi-finals. A 1-0 home win and a 1-1 draw at Anfield (both Forest goals were John Robertson penalties) was enough to put Forest into the final against Wolverhampton Wanderers.

As European Cup winners, Forest faced Barcelona (the Cup Winners' Cup Winners) in the Super Cup Final. The first leg at The City Ground was won 1-0 when on-loan Charlie George scored the only goal. In Spain the trophy was secured with a 1-1 draw, when Kenny Burns scored (opposite). The Reds won even though John Robertson missed a penalty. Stan Bowles remembers the night as being the only trophy he won in his entire professional career.

[next page] Brian Clough and Peter Taylor leave Wembley after Forest had failed in their bid for a third successive League Cup Final, losing 1-0 to Wolverhampton Wanderers. The Reds had numerous chances but a mix-up between David Needham and Peter Shilton gifted the West Midlanders the only goal.

Europapokal der Landesmeister
Viertelfinale   Rückspiel

BFC Dynamo –
        Nottingham Forest

PROGRAMM

Mittwoch, 19. März 1980, 18.00 Uhr
Friedrich - Ludwig - Jahn - Sportpark   0,50 M

Dynamo Berlin celebrate the only goal of the European Cup quarter-final first leg at The City Ground in March 1980. Against the odds the Reds managed a 3-1 away win, with two Trevor Francis goals, to battle into the last four.

officieel programma   prijs ƒ 0,90

ajax -
nottingham forest

return
halve finale
europa cup I

seizoen 1979-1980

no. 35

unique uitzendburo
bel de unique hotline
020-236545

Forest met the giants of Ajax in the European Cup semi-final. The Dutch side had won the trophy three times in the 1970s and were led by World Cup star Rudi Krol (seen here exchanging pennants with John McGovern). Forest produced an assured display at The City Ground and gained an important 2-0 advantage. In Holland Ajax put the Reds under a lot of pressure but could only score once.

REAL FEDERACION ESPAÑOLA DE FUTBOL

ESTADIO SANTIAGO BERNABEU
FINAL COPA DE EUROPA DE CLUBS CAMPEONES DE LIGA (XXV EDICION)
28 mayo 1980 - A las 20,30 horas - NOTTINGHAM FOREST F.C. - HAMBURGER SPORT-VEREIN

12

Entrada de Fondo Norte
PLANTA BAJA - DE PIE

Nº 0974

500 ptas.

ENTRADA

PUERTA
39

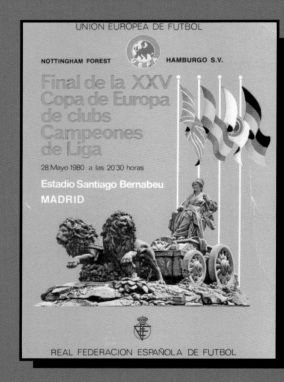

UNION EUROPEA DE FUTBOL

NOTTINGHAM FOREST   HAMBURGO S.V.

Final de la XXV
Copa de Europa
de clubs
Campeones
de Liga

28 Mayo 1980 a las 20'30 horas

Estadio Santiago Bernabeu
MADRID

REAL FEDERACION ESPAÑOLA DE FUTBOL

The 1980 European Cup Final was staged in Madrid between Forest and Hamburg, who featured Kevin Keegan.

Peter Shilton takes a catch while Viv Anderson looks on.

Ian Bowyer stands aside as John Robertson fires in a shot . . . which turned out to be the game's only goal.

FROM THE Reds' hideaway in the Spanish hills Peter Taylor described the game as Forest's finest hour. He said: "It was a performance of the highest order and there is no comparison in the achievement this year against the one last year.

"Hamburg are a side of real quality and class and we had to show something really special to win this one but we felt confident before the start and even though they forced us to defend we always felt that we could do it.

REDS FINEST HOUR — TAYLOR

Forest 1   Hamburg 0

JOHN ROBERTSON, the Munich goal-maker, became the Madrid goal-taker as Forest defied the vast majority of predictions to retain their European crown.

The Scot, who could not have had a more fitting finale to his testimonial season, struck in the 20th minute of a game in which Forest soaked up punishment like never before.

But they dragged their weary limbs through the most painful barriers to make sure of another never to be forgotten milestone in the history of the club.

Not for the first time — but certainly on the biggest occasion — Forest leant so heavily on their reserves of courage and character that you felt they would surely buckle. But to even suggest that is a slur on a side who relish defying the odds just as much as they love winning trophies.

Shilton

Before the game, the players knew that Hamburg would provide them with their sternest European challenge but their feelings were epitomised in the words of Martin O'Neill, who missed out on last year's crowning glory.

"We know what we are up against," he said. "But we will give absolutely everything and if we happen to score we will run all night long." That, in a short but decisive declaration, is what Forest proceeded to do. And O'Neill's exhausting contribution typified the overall effort.

There were the breathtaking saves of Peter Shilton, the defensive power of Kenny Burns, the long and lonely running of Garry Birtles . . . everywhere you looked you could pick out a hero in red.

But the lasting glamour descended on Robertson.

from John Lawson in Madrid

He left Manny Kaltz, the man who many pundits said would be the match-winner himself, groping before playing a one-two with Birtles and squeezing a right foot shot inside the post.

It gave Forest enormous strength for the continuing battle but there were moments of real anguish — as in the very next minute when Reimann shot home but had the effort ruled out for off-side.

And the Germans could hardly believe their eyes when Shilton produced those saves of world class to deny Magath Milewski and Nogly.

With Kaltz driving one of his renowned "bolts" into the outside of the post, there was no shortage of palpitations. But Forest's heartbeat grew stronger.

And it was positively racing when O'Neill played Birtles clear in 87th minute. But his legs could not carry him through for the second goal that Forest had so desperately needed for an hour or more.

Regardless, they hung on for the most memorable of victories. But with this side and this management it will almost certainly be overtaken at some stage in the future.

Man of the Match
Kenny Burns

Frank Gray, goal scorer John Robertson and John O'Hare, who came on as substitute celebrate in the changing rooms.

Martin O'Neill, Frank Gray (with the cup) and Garry Birtles rejoice after a great win.

Another great save as Peter Shilton denies the Hamburg attackers.

Viv Anderson and Kenny Burns keep up their tireless work in defence.

[previous page] Forest were drawn against CSKA Sofia in the first round of the 1980-81 European Cup. Here John Robertson goes close in the first-leg, a shock 1-0 away defeat.

The home-leg was even more shocking. Forest lost 1-0 again and the European champions went out at the first hurdle. The stunned look on John Robertson's face tells the whole story.

[opposite page] Garry Birtles was the next Forest star to leave as he was sold to Manchester United for over £1 million.

ropean Cup action ★ European Cup

NIGHTMARE END TO THE DREAM RIDE

FOREST 0, CSKA SOFIA 1

Report by

Tomisaburo Hirai, President of the Football Association of Japan,
and
Seishi Kato, Chairman of Toyota Motor Sales Co., Ltd.,
cordially invite you to attend The Toyota European/South American Cup soccer game
on Wednesday, February 11, 1981, at the National Stadium in Tokyo.
The match will be played between
Nottingham Forest Football Club of England
(1980 European Champion Clubs' Cup champion)
and
Club Nacional de Football of Uruguay
(1980 Copa Libertadores champion).
Gates will open at 9:00 a.m. and kickoff is scheduled at 12:00 noon.
You are advised to arrive by 11:30 a.m.
One invitation will allow you and your wife only.

R.S.V.P. [Please use the enclosed postcard to notify us of your attendance.
We may not be able to secure your seat otherwise.]

[opposite] As Forest began rebuilding the squad the likes of Peter Ward (pictured), Justin Fashanu and Ian Wallace were all signed.

[below] In February 1981 Forest travelled for the first World Club Championship game to be held in Tokyo against Nacional Montevideo of Uruguay.

NO. 02650

TOYOTA
EUROPEAN/SOUTH AMERICAN
CUP

世界一決定戦... サッカーが語れる日がやってくる。

'81 2月11日(祝)

トヨタ ヨーロッパ／サウス アメリカ カップ
ノッティンガム・フォレスト(イングランド)
VS
ナシオナル・モンテビデオ(ウルグァイ)
場所／東京・国立競技場　キックオフ／12時

S 席

門GATE	入口ENTRANCE	ブロックBLOCK	席SE.AT
千駄ヶ谷 代々木	5	後段 C	40

催：国際サッカー連盟(FIFA)／ヨーロッパサッカー連盟(UEFA)／南アメリカサッカー連盟(CONMEBOL)　主管：(財)日本サッカー協会　後援：トヨタ自動車

NOTTINGHAM FOREST

ピーター・シルトン

GK
イングランド代表
身長182ギン
体重81ギ
31歳

世界最高クラスのゴールキーパー。1977年にストーク・シティから移籍。以後ノッティンガムの数々のタイトル獲得になくてはならない男となった。欠点のないGKだ。

ビブ・アンダーソン

DF
（右バック）
イングランド代表
身長179ギン
体重65ギ
24歳

黒人選手として初めてイングランド代表になったライトバック。長い足を生かした守備も定評があるが、すばらしいスピードとドリブルを生かした攻撃参加は迫力充分だ。

ケニー・バーンズ

DF
（スイーパー）
スコットランド代表
身長178ギン
体重70ギ
27歳

1977～78年シーズンのイングランド最優秀選手。77年にバーミンガムから移籍し、ノッティンガムではもっぱらスイーパーだが、バーミンガム時代はMFやFWもこなし、得点力も高い。

ラリー・ロイド

DF
（ストッパー）
イングランド代表
身長187ギン
体重78ギ
32歳

リバプールで活躍したストッパー。コベントリーを経て76年にノッティンガム入り。その後の活躍はすばらしく、エースキラーとして、80年にはイングランド代表に呼び戻された。

フランキー・グレイ

DF
（左バック）
スコットランド代表
身長176ギン
体重74ギ
26歳

スコットランド代表でもレギュラーのレフトバック。リーズから移った選手だが、かつてのスコットランド代表の名左ウイング、エディ・グレイの弟だけに攻撃力はすばらしい。

デービッド・ニーダム

DF
（ストッパー）
身長185ギン
体重79ギ

バックラインの控え選手。77年12月、ロイドの負傷中にQPRから買われた。イングランドのB代表にも選ばれたが、ノッティンガムではまだレギュラーではない。

ブリン・ガン

DF
（右バック）
身長176ギン
体重66ギ

最近頭角を現してきた若手のサイドバック。まだ交代出場が多いが、80年5月の欧州カップ決勝でも、10分間プレーした。ダービー生まれで、ノッティンガムが育てた将来の中心選手だ。

ジョン・マクガバン

MF
身長177ギン
体重69ギ
31歳

キャプテン。20年間、4つのクラブをクラブ監督とともに渡り歩き、400を超すリーグ戦に出場。鉄の意志力をもったプロフェッショナルだ。スコットランド代表からもれているのは不思議。

ゲーリー・ミルズ

MF
身長172ギン
体重70ギ
19歳

クラブの最も有望な若手。78年に16歳でデビューし、今季はもうレギュラー。少年時代はサッカーとともにラグビーでもイングランド・スクールボーイ代表だった。

イアン・ボイヤー

MF
スコットランド代表
身長179ギン
体重71ギ

73年にオリエントから移籍。得点力のあるMFとして重要な存在。オールラウンドな能力をもった選手で、どのポジションもこなす。GKのサブとしてプレーしたこともある。

ジョン・ロバートソン

MF
スコットランド代表
身長172ギン
体重67ギ
28歳

ずんぐりとした体つきで、けっしてスマートとはいえないが、中盤から左ウイングの位置へ出ていくときの威力は欧州有数。80年チャンピオンズ・カップのヒーローだ。

ライモンド・ポンテ

MF
スイス代表
身長177ギン
体重76ギ
25歳

ナポリ生まれのスイス人。今季途中、スイスのグラスホッパーから移籍、まだレギュラーポジションはつかんでいないが、これからの中盤のリーダーとして期待を集めている。

トレバー・フランシス

FW
イングランド代表
身長177ギン
体重73ギ
26歳

イングランド・サッカー界の貴公子。79年2月に英国史上初の100万ポンドでバーミンガムから移籍され、その年5月の欧州カップ決勝で貴重な1点を決めた。長い負傷から最近復調。

ピーター・ワード

FW
イングランド代表
身長170ギン
体重65ギ

80年秋にブライトンから補強された若手のストライカー。小柄だがスピードに乗った動きが売り物で、ブライトンでも得点王。ブライトンを3部から1部へ急上昇させた立役者だ。

イアン・ウォレス

FW
スコットランド代表
身長171ギン
体重68ギ
24歳

コベントリーの一員として78年にも来日した赤毛のインテリ・ストライカー。今季そのコベントリーから買われたが、ウォレスはフランシスに次ぐクラブ史上2人目の100万ポンド選手となった。

マーチン・オニール

FW
北アイルランド代表
身長177ギン
体重67ギ

ベルファストの大学で法学を修めたインテリ。右のウイングですばらしい技巧とスピードを披露する。北アイルランド代表チームでは、最近キャプテンに選ばれている。

TIME OF SUBSTITUTION TIEMPO DE CAMBIO	SHOOTS CHUTES EXTRA TIME PROLOGA	2ND HALF 2º TIEMPO	1ST HALF 1er TIEMPO	PLAYERS JUGADORES	NO.	POSITION POSICION	NO.	PLAYERS JUGADORES	1ST HALF 1er TIEMPO	2ND HALF 2º TIEMPO	EXTRA TIME PROLOGA	TIME OF SUBSTITUTION
MIN.				SHILTON	1	G K	1	RODRIGUES				MIN.
		/	/	ANDERSON	2	D F	2	MOREIRA				
				F. GRAY	3	"	4	BLANCO				
	/ /			S. GRAY	15	"	3	EVRIQUEZ				
				LLOYD	5	"	5	GONZALEZ				
	/			BURNS	6	M F	8	MILAR	/ /			
		/	/	O'NEIL	7	"	6	ESPARRAGO				
22 MIN		/	/	PONTE	8	"	10	LUZARDO	/	/		
				FRANCIS	9	F W	7	BICA				
	/ /		/	WALLACE	10	"	9	VICTORINO	/	/ /	X	
		/	/	ROBERTSON	11	"	11	MORALES				

SUBSTITUES SUPLENTES / 交代要員 SUBSTITUES SÚPLENTES / SUBSTITUES SUPLENTES

		/ /		WARD	12		12	PEREIRA				
				NEEDHAM	13		13	MOLINA				
							14	W. CABRERA				
							18	J. CABRERA				
							19	PEREZ				

NOTE NOTAS	TOTAL	2ND HALF 2º TIEMPO	1ST HALF 1er TIEMPO		1ST HALF 1er TIEMPO	2ND HALF 2º TIEMPO	TOTAL	NOTE NOTAS
	5	1	4	G K	7	11	18	
CAUTION TARJETA AMARILLA	7	3	4	C K	1	1	2	CAUTION TARJETA AMARILLA
⑤ 77 MIN	23 35	6	17	DIRECT FK 直排FK TIRO LIBRE DIRECTO	11	12	23 26	⑥ 25 min.
	12	6	6	INDIRECT FK 間排FK TIRO LIBRE INDIRECTO	2	1	3	
	0	0	0	P K	0	0	0	

GOALS GOLES	MARK SIGLAS	DRIBBLE REGATEO ~ドリブル	GROUNDER PASS RASO →ゴロのパス	FLOATING & LOW PASS ROMBEO 浮球のパス	MIX-UP LUCHA X混戦	SHOOT CHUTE S シュート	HEADING CABECEO H ヘディング	SCORER GOLEADOR 得点者名	ASSIST ASISTENTE アシスト者名
10 MIN	③ ~ → ① S		(NACIONAL)					VICTORINO	MOREIRA

The Forest team and the referees report from the game in Tokyo. The number of shots highlights Forest's domination of the match, but they lost 1-0.

Ian Wallace tangles with Ipswich's Terry Butcher in an FA Cup replay at Portman Road. Forest reached the quarter-finals but were held 3-3 at The City Ground before losing the replay 1-0.

Kenny Burns is sent off during a pre-season game in Spain.

Brian Clough found himself in sole charge at The City Ground when Peter Taylor retired. However Taylor then took the manager's job at Derby County.

[above] Ian Bowyer, Steve Wigley, Bryn Gunn and Colin Walsh try out the latest in video game technology, October 1982.

[below] Mark Proctor, Bryn Gunn, Gary Mills, Colin Walsh and Stuart Gray do some promotional gardening.

[above] Ian Bowyer celebrates Paul Hart's late 'goal' versus Anderlecht in the 1984 UEFA Cup semi-final. The effort was disallowed and Forest went out 3-2 on aggregate.

[below] Awards night 1986. Nigel Clough, Neil Webb, Des Walker, Barbara Clough, Johnny Metgod and chairman Fred Reacher.

Garry Birtles returned to Forest in 1982. Here he scores against Manchester United at The City Ground in October 1986.

FEDERACION GUIPUZCOANA DE FUTBOL

COMITE NACIONAL DE ARBITROS

TEMPORADA 19 85 - 19 86   CAMPEONATO AMISTOSO

ACTA del partido celebrado el 15 de ABRIL , en SAN SEBASTIAN

Clubs { REAL SOCIEDAD , de "
       { NOTTINGHAN FOREST , de

Campo ATOTXA

Arbitro: D. JOAQUIN URIO VELAZQUEZ , del Colegio de GUIPUZCOA

Juez de línea: D. ALFREDO MANGADO NAVARLAZ , de "

Juez de línea: D. XABIER ELEICEGUI URANGA , de "

Equipo REAL SOCIEDAD		Equipo NOTTINGHAM FOREST
(Escríbase con letras MAYUSCULAS)		
1	ELDUAYEN	1	SUTTON
2	SAGARZAZU	2	BUTTERWORTH
3	SUKIA	3	PEARCE
4	LARRAÑAGA	4	WALKER
5	GORRIZ	5	METGOD
6	ALBISTEGI	6	RICE
7	ZURILLAGA	7	CARR
8	MUJIKA	8	WEBB
9	URALDE	9	BIRTLES
10	ZAMORA	10	CAMPBELL D.
11	LOPEZ UFARTE	11	WALSH

COMPETICION REGIONAL (watermark)

Jugadores Suplentes

12	BEGUIRISTAIN 16- DADIE	12	CLOUGH
13	ARANGUREN 17- URBIETA	13	FLEMING
14	LOREN	14 15	BOWYER
15	BENGOETXEA	15 16	CAMPBELL R.

Entrenador D. .... Lic. n.º ....   Entrenador D. .... Lic. n.º ....

Auxiliar D. .... Lic. n.º ....   Auxiliar D. .... Lic. n.º ....

Resultado { REAL SOCIEDAD = CERO (0)
           { NOTTINGHAN FOREST = TRES (3)

Hora comienzo { 1.ª parte 8 0h
               { 2.ª parte 8 0b. 55'

El Capitán y Entrenador del REAL SOCIEDAD N.º

El Capitán y Entrenador del NOTTINGHAN FOREST N.º 5

El D.º de Campo D. IÑAKI SARRIEGUI OYANEDER

SAN SEBASTIAN a 15 de ABRIL de 198 6

El Arbitro,

El acta original para la Federación Guipuzcoana se enviará inmediatamente por el primer correo; y las copias para los Clubs, se entregarán a los Delegados de los mismos, una vez terminado el partido en el propio campo.

[above] Brian Clough shows exactly how he wants it done.

[below] Forest were still going for four trophies in March 1989. They were third in the League had won through to both the League Cup and Simod Cup Finals. They were drawn away to Manchester United in the quarter-finals of the FA Cup where Franz Carr set-up Garry Parker for the only goal of the game and here we see Steve Sutton and John Motson reviewing a goal-line clearace after the match.

After a gap of nine years Forest returned to winning trophies with the 1989 League Cup. Nigel Clough scores a penalty, above, and Neil Webb (below) celebrates his goal in the 3-1 win over Luton Town.

[opposite] Stuart Pearce and Steve Sutton with the League Cup at Wembley.

Brian Clough salutes the fans after Forest had just beaten Oldham Athletic 1-0 at Wembley to claim their second consecutive League Cup win.

Roy Keane brought an aggressive element to the Forest midfield in the early 1990s. Here he is in action against West Ham's Ian Bishop.

Having lost FA Cup semi-finals in 1988 and 1989, the Reds won one in 1991. West Ham were on the end of a 4-0 beating at Villa Park. The second-half goals flew in from (top to bottom); Gary Crosby, Roy Keane, Stuart Pearce and Gary Charles.

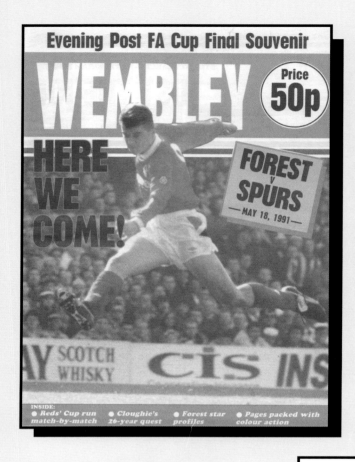

Evening Post FA Cup Final Souvenir

WEMBLEY

Price
50p

HERE WE COME!

FOREST
v
SPURS
— MAY 18, 1991 —

...AY SCOTCH WHISKY   CIS INS...

INSIDE:
● Reds' Cup run match-by-match   ● Cloughie's 26-year quest   ● Forest star profiles   ● Pages packed with colour action

Forest reached Wembley finals six times between 1989 and 1992; three League Cup Finals, one FA Cup Finals, one Zenith Data Systems Cup Final and a Simod Cup Final.

FA CUP FINAL

NOTTINGHAM FOREST
V
TOTTENHAM HOTSPUR

AT WEMBLEY STADIUM
SATURDAY 18th MAY 1991

Forest

EXECUTIVE TRAIN
MENU

Reg. Office:
City Ground
Nottingham NG2 5FJ

Reg. in England No. 1630402

Telephone 822202
Information Desk 821122
Commercial Dept. 820444

Telegrams:
Forestball Nottingham

Manager:
Brian H. Clough, M.A., O.B.E.

Commercial Manager:
David A. Pullan

NOTTINGHAM FOREST
Football Club Ltd.

FOUNDED 1865

Directors:
M. Roworth (Chairman)
J.F. Hickling (Jt. Vice-Chairman)
I.I. Korn (Jt. Vice-Chairman)
G.E. Macpherson, J.P.
F. Reacher
J.M. Smith
C. Wootton
G.W. Waterhouse, B.Sc., Ph.D., C.Eng.

Secretary:
Paul White

Our Ref: DP/AHR   Your Ref:

CITY GROUND
NOTTINGHAM NG2 5FJ

18th March, 1992.

Dear Sir/Madam,

Zenith Data Systems Cup Final
Executive Train - Sunday 29th March, 1992.
Nottingham Forest v Southampton - kick-off 3.00 p.m.

Please find enclosed your train ticket/s together with the Nottingham Forest boarding pass relative to the above game.

Set out below are details of the day's itinerary.

a)   The train will leave Nottingham Midland Station at 10.15 a.m. It is anticipated that we will depart from platform one although this is not confirmed.   Please enter the station through the main entrance; you will observe a large notice informing you of the platform number.

b)   Car parking at the station is not guaranteed; however, British Rail now operate a pay and display policy.

c)   On each carriage there will be two stewards and each carriage will be clearly marked with a letter.   You will see from the Nottingham Forest boarding pass your carriage letter and seat number, followed by a letter B or F.   This means you are travelling with your <u>Back</u> to the engine or facing <u>Frontwards</u>.   Any queries should be directed to your steward.

d)   You will be issued with your match ticket on the train by your stewards.   This is in order to avoid any panic over the travellers either losing or forgetting their tickets on the day.

e)   On arriving at Wembley Central, the stadium is approximately a 15 minutes casual walk away.

f)   We depart from Wembley Central at 6.15 p.m. and you would be advised to be at the station by 5.45 at the latest and then follow the same procedure as outlined above.

g)   We have endeavoured to obtain permission to serve alcohol on the train but the Police Authorities and our legal advisors inform us that it is not possible to either serve or for passengers to take alcohol on this train.

Should you have any queries regarding these arrangements please do not hesitate to contact me. I sincerely hope you have an enjoyable day with us and, of course, we get the right result.

Yours sincerely,

David Pullan

David A. Pullan. Commercial Manager.

European Cup: 1978/79, 1979/80; Football League Division I: Champions 1977/78, Runners-up 1966/67, 1978/79; Football League Cup: Winners 1977/78, 1978/79, Finalists 1979/80; Littlewoods Cup: Winners 1988/89, 1989/90; F.A. Cup: Winners 1898, 1959; Anglo-Scottish Competition: Winners 1976/77; Simod Cup: Winners 1988/89; European Super Competition: Winners 1979/80, Finalists 1980/81; World Club Championship: Finalists 1980/81

Teddy Sheringham scores the winning goal against Liverpool in the first live Sky TV game of the newly formed Premiership in 1992. It was a poor season though and Brian Clough announced his retirement as Forest were relegated.

Stan Collymore's flying header was enough to beat Notts County at The City Ground as Forest bounced straight back to the Premiership at the first time of asking in 1993-94.

Mark Crossley kept 10 clean sheets in 36 league games as Forest gained automatic promotion.

Forest stunned Sheffield Wednesday 7-1 at Hillsborough on April 1st 1995. It capped a fine season back in the top flight as Forest finished third in the Premiership and qualified for Europe.

FOREST HAVE THE CLASS TO WIN CUP

UEFA Cup conqueror Bryan Roy believes Nottingham Forest have the talent to bring him a second winners medal — if they can cope with the stamina-sapping schedule of the English game.

If they can take pace in Premier

Roy's marvellous goal against Malmo at the City Ground last night guaranteed Forest's participation in Friday's draw for the second round.

The Dutch international finished on the winning side with Ajax four years ago and knows exactly what is required to succeed in the competition.

He is convinced that Forest have a squad gifted enough to compete with giants like AC Milan, Barcelona, Bayern Munich and Benfica.

But he feels that English teams face a tougher task than any other European sides in winning what is the most difficult of the three major trophies because of the heavy schedule of matches they are forced to play.

"We have the talent at Forest to win the competition. We have the players who are skilful and experienced to compete with the best in Europe," said Roy.

"But the big problem we have is that we have to play so many games in a season. To win the competition will be harder for us or any other English team than anyone else, because no one else in Europe plays 60 matches in a season.

"It's hard to produce your very best form week in and week out. That's not

By IAN EDWARDS

headed Woan's centre straight at Jonnie Fedel. Eventually, when the goal came, it was by the simplest of routes.

Mark Crossley's huge clearance was missed by Jorgen Ohlsson and Roy collected the loose ball and struck a vicious shot high into the roof of the net as Fedel could only stand and watch.

"It was a magnificent goal. A marvellous strike. I said before the game that Bryan can be our matchwinner on his own and he proved it," said Clark.

"I just wish he had stuck one or two of the other chances in as well. It

FOREST 1, MALMO 0

FOREST: Crossley, Lyttle, Pearce, Cooper, Chettle, Stone, Bart-Williams, Bohinen (Gemmill 88), Roy (Silenzi 88), Lee, Woan. Not used: Clark, Tiler, McGregor.

MALMO: Fedel, Nylen, T Persson, Wirmola, Ohlsson, J Persson, O Andersson (Dahlstrom 76), Prytz, K Andersson, Petersson, Fjellstrom (Olsson 80). Not used: Nilsson, Thylander, Olofsson.

GOAL FOR: Forest — Roy (70mins).

GOAL ATTEMPTS ON TARGET: Forest 8, Malmo 3

GOAL ATTEMPTS OFF TARGET: Forest 7, Malmo 3

Bryan Roy's goal edged Forest through in the UEFA Cup against Malmo. Auxerre and Lyon (Bobby Howe and Paul MacGregor in action below) were also defeated before the Reds bowed out to Bayern Munich in the quarter-finals.

After being relegated again in 1997, Dave Bassett guided Forest to the First Division Championship in 1997-98. Back row, left to right: Des Lyttle, Paul MacGregor, Kevin Campbell, Geoff Thomas, Jon Olav Hjelde, Andy Johnson, Steve Stone. Middle row, left to right; John Haselden (physio), Craig Armstrong, Steve Chettle, Marco Pascolo, Dave Beasant, Mark Crossley, Steve Guinan, Ian Moore, Liam O'Kane (coach), Mike Kelly. Front row, left to right; Scott Gemmill, Thierry Bonalair, Pierre van Hooijdonk, Colin Cooper, Dave Bassett (manager), Chris Bart-Williams, Ian Woan, Alan Rogers.

The 21st Century

By 2003 it was all change at The City Ground. Forest had been relegated to the second tier once again and now Paul Hart was in charge. He utilised many players that he'd worked with at the Forest Academy and the likes of Michael Dawson (below), Andy Reid, David Prutton, Jermaine Jenas and Marlon Harewood were given their chance. In 2003 Forest made it to the play-offs before losing a memorable match at Bramall Lane 4-3 after extra-time.

David Johnson (right) was signed from Ipswich Town and provided 29 goals in the play-off season. Injuries then hampered the rest of his Forest career but he returned to score five goals in he last four games of the 2003-04 season when Forest were battling against relegation.

Marlon King (below) scored an emotional winner against West Ham at The City Ground on September 26th 2004, the first home game after the death of Brian Clough.

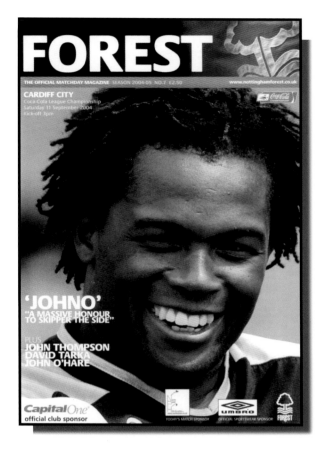

NOTTINGHAM'S GREATEST LEGENDS

EVENING POST

Established 1878

Saturday May 19, 2007   35p   Visit our website www.thisisnottingham.co.uk

LITTLE STARS

Voting form: Page 12

Crying shame
Forest slump 5-2

Agony as Reds lose to Yeovil in the play-offs: Pages 10&11 and 40-44

INSIDE: Weather 4 ● Letters 14&15 ● Business 19 ● EG Daily 23 ● Sport 28-44

Bobbers Mill
Blaze fumes scare

TRICK blaze fumes filled the air and homes were hit last night as a blaze ripped through a factory site.

Fire crews were called to the blaze in the afternoon to put out the flames at the former Wicking Flooring plant site in Bobbers Mill Road.

The flames were seen in the early afternoon in between the units, which are mainly used as storage warehouses.

Continued: Page 2

West Bridgford
Cancer cash battle

A FORMER council worker who is dying of an asbestos-related cancer has launched a legal battle for up to £200,000 compensation.

Geoffrey Hewitt, of Risho Road, West Bridgford, is suing from Nottingham his former employers, Nottingham City Council.

Mr Hewitt, 75, developed mesothelioma, a cancer of the lining of the lungs, after being exposed to a writ in London's High Court.

Full story: Page 5

Carrington
Drugs raid warning

LANDLORDS are being warned to mind their properties repeatedly after police raided an address including cannabis plants with a street value of thousands of pounds.

Police found rooms containing the class C drug in a Carrington house last week.

Landlords are being advised to be on their guard. Police say if they turn out homes to their property in order. They should make a unit.

Full story: Page 17

More than 100 years at the heart of the action...

FOOTBALL POST
An edition of the   NOTTINGHAM EVENING POST, Saturday May 19, 2007, No. 45, Vol. LXXXVI   60p

DREAM IS OVER

Forest knocked out
of play-offs by Yeovil

Match report: Page 5
Fans' reaction: Back Page

Take that: Forest's Robert Earnshaw celebrates his goal against Manchester City – leaving Mark Hughes's future at Eastlands in serious doubt. Photographs by Nigel Roddis/Reuters; Jon Super/AP.

FOREST FIRE

Mark Hughes on the brink as mega-rich Manchester City are humiliated by Championship strugglers Nottingham Forest – whose new manager Billy Davies watched from the stands. City 0 Forest 3, plus the rest of the FA Cup third round: pages 2-7

Forest were back in the Championship for the 2008-09 campaign and scored a memorable 3-0 away win at Manchester City in the FA Cup.

[opposite] With Billy Davies installed as manager, Forest made nine new signings during the summer of 2009.

[following pages] The 2009-2010 squad picture / Celebrations on August 29th 2009 as Forest beat Derby County 3-2 at The City Ground.

Official Matchday Magazine 2009-10 Issue 04 £3

forest

the new recruits

Introducing Billy's nine
summer signings

Coca-Cola Championship
Saturday August 15
Kick-off 3pm
West Bromwich Albion

FOREST

Subscribers

1	NFFC	51	Stephen Purdy
2	Nigel Doughty	52	Paul Terence Weatherbed
3	Rob Jovanovic	53	Rupert Bellamy
4	Gino Farabella	54	Glyn Chamberlain
5	Francis Eizens	55	Peter Mitchell
6	Anthony Beecroft	56	Giles Colin
7	Geoff Peabody	57	Jerry Ellis
8	Fraser Nicholson	58	Keith N. Kingscott
9	Mark Arthur	59	Tony Walker
10	Brandon Furse	60	Dave Sterry
11	Milan Jovanovic	61	Hugh Brennan
12	John Lawson	62	Robin M. Morris
13	Dave Brown (Plymouth Red)	63	Martin Chell
14	Steve Nicklin "Schnookie"	64	Philip West
15	Dr Neil Whittemore	65	David Fraser
16	Mike Haywood	66	Jacques Ransford
17	Karl Jovanovic	67	Mark Jackson
18	Suzanne Jovanovic	68	D. R. Reavill
19	Tony Farabella	69	Simon Wetherill
20	Lou Farabella	70	Robert Phillips
21	Mike West	71	Neil R. Smith
22	Taylor Louise West	72	Jason Simpkins
23	Lance Darlaston	73	Robert Johnson (Bob)
24	Paul White	74	Andy & Tracy Francis
25	Wim Van Walle	75	Phil Aldridge
26	Ken Smales	76	James Parnham
27	Charity Donation	77	Tim Clarke
28	Charity Donation	78	Alan, Alice & Emily Bryant
29	University of Nottingham	79	Phil Wilson
30	Mick Ellis	80	Karen Arnold
31	Stewart Byas	81	Richard Green
32	Alan Merryweather	82	Andrew Findlay
33	Crispin Morton (Bridport Red)	83	David Wilkins
34	Stephen Hayes	84	Liam Lown
35	Simon T Jarvis	85	Robert F MacArthur
36	Nigel Fish	86	Peter R Mitchell
37	Michael Helme	87	Philip Barber
38	David Bingham	88	Dave Peel
39	Simon Bingham	89	Ian Copping
40	Thomas Cundy	90	David Price
41	Paul Leslie Henton	91	A W Grocock
42	Darren Rigley	92	Phil Sheldon
43	Keith Rigg	93	Kevin Daybell
44	Mr Paul C Clifford	94	Neil Pickworth
45	Doug Sutton	95	Richard Macer
46	Martin Pullon	96	Stuart Kaye
47	Anthony and Margaret Ford	97	Mr Ian Clarke (Skip)
48	Steve Tring	98	Cherrie Holmes & Paul Simmons
49	Clive Hallam	99	John Shelley
50	Stephen Hallam	100	Terry Hall

101	Brian Bernard Olbison	151	Ivan Rockley
102	Stephen Groves	152	John Nightingale
103	Simon Covell	153	Mat Lamb
104	Philip Coates	154	Simon Edward Powers
105	Barry and Jake Clarke	155	Robert Severn
106	Mark Jopling	156	Richard Gadsby
107	Brown Family	157	Phil Reynolds
108	Roger Peter Towle	158	Scott Davies
109	Adrian J Taylor	159	Gary Hall
110	Alan Spencer	160	Andy Linley
111	Richard "Rich B" Burgess	161	Richard Bullett
112	Steven Naylor	162	John and Aline Oliver
113	Phil Slater	163	Paul Wood
114	David Shaw	164	Nick Houldsworth
115	Jonathon Clarke	165	Nick Bowler
116	Richard H Harrison	166	Thomas Newton
117	Charles Wheeler	167	David Charles Mills
118	Darren Paul Nunn, Nathan Adam Forest Nunn	168	Mr Nicholas Oskiewicz
119	Rowland Buchanan	169	Adam Scott Cook
120	Phillip Wass	170	Pauline Wilkinson
121	Nicholas Parker	171	Ian Walker
122	Frank Cooke	172	Peter Harvey
123	Trevor M Smith	173	David Lloyd
124	Steve Bateman	174	James Pollard
125	John Simpson	175	Steven P Williams
126	Richard Patching	176	Adam Chantrey
127	D J Beaumont	177	Gareth Banton
128	Simon Ray	178	Tony Wintle
129	Paul Baldock	179	Roy Hardstaff
130	Jonathon David Coleflax	180	Wayne Andrew Martin
131	Grenville Jennings	181	Tristan Squire
132	Les Bolam	182	The Browns
133	Kjetil Hågenvik	183	Luke Rigg
134	Martin Paul Hackett	184	Peter Rogers
135	Andrew Terry	185	Peter James Smith
136	David Read	186	Michael John Gascoigne
137	Keir Robinson	187	Paul Rennie
138	Chris Ingle	188	Craig Brandom
139	Roy Mullin	189	John Rowland
140	Ian Foston	190	Jonathan Buttery
141	Jonathan Rushby	191	Peter Gibson
142	Keith Hardy	192	Miles Appleby
143	Nigel Newbold	193	Paul Johnson
144	David Gareth Barker	194	Christopher Brown
145	Margaret and Melvin Clarke	195	Bill Barnes
146	David Rowley	196	John Gretton
147	Paul Johnson	197	Tim Farr
148	Mike Woodman	198	Tom Farr
149	Michael Beardsmore	199	Beth Farr
150	Gary Lambert	200	Will Farr

201	David and Nick Long
202	Donald Wright
203	Alex Dutton
204	Mick Jones
205	John Frank Baker & Graham Baker
206	Ray Wilson
207	Rich Fisher
208	Steve Waterfield
209	Mark Beers
210	Ian Filby
211	Mick Wyer
212	Mr Christopher Bryan Corke
213	Neil
214	Richard Stenhouse
215	Alan Poole
216	Tim Gabb
217	Debbie Roberts
218	Terence Whitehead
219	Andrew and Jackie Smith
220	Stephen Rawlinson
221	Nick Pritchett
222	David John Dewar
223	David Stainsby
224	R. Edward Waring
225	Robert Middleton Happy 50th Birthday
226	Michael Ewers
227	John Ringrose
228	Alan Hutson
229	Corby MacDonald
230	Alan E Barker
231	Adam Wimbledon
232	Georgie Bargel
233	Grenvill Sisson
234	Mr Gerard Michael Paul Milano
235	Peter David Stanton
236	Adam Lea Wilkins
237	Malcolm Fox
238	Paul Allen
239	Thomas Allen
240	Kevin Neill
241	Robert Henry Cummings
242	John Cottee
243	James E Mellors
244	Dominic Smith
245	George H Rose
246	Ashley Smith
247	Neil Patrick
248	Raymond John Vardy
249	Alan Imms
250	Ralph Bates
251	John Samuel
252	Paul Carpenter
253	Darren Smith
254	P. C. G. Heaton
255	Steve White
256	Richard Stocken
257	Mr Trevor Stevenson
258	John Lomax
259	Daniel Radford
260	Lee Dillon
261	Jim Williams
262	Simon Grant
263	Arthur Edward Brozych
264	Mark Morris
265	Craig Spiby
266	David Hull
267	Simon Amess
268	Michael Anthony Woolley
269	Peter Raeburn
270	Simon Hunt
271	The Hunt Family
272	James Bradley
273	Nidge Barnard
274	James Plumb
275	Neil Marshall
276	David T Carrington
277	Dave Pearce
278	Brendon McCabe
279	Chris Brewer
280	Gwyn Edwards
281	Dean Walton
282	Christopher D Bowron
283	Lev Piddubriwnyj
284	Roman Semak
285	David Shorto
286	Anthony Smith
287	Stephen Polkey
288	Steve Wright
289	-
290	Jamie Hinchliffe
291	Anne Walters
292	Philip Walters
293	Adrian Walters
294	John Bodsworth - 20th Sep 1975
295	Robin Dale
296	Keith FJ Shillingford
297	Paul Chambers
298	Mark G Morris
299	Pete Turton
300	Gareth Higginbottom

301	Stephen Jolley
302	Gary Hopewell
303	Graham A Davison
304	B Baker
305	John Charles Spencer
306	Alan J Sinden
307	Dave Tarry
308	Gary Atkinson
309	Graham R A Irving
310	Geoff Brookes
311	Dave Bloor
312	David Armitage - Nottingham Forest supporter man & boy Happy 40th Birthday
313	Stewart Hague
314	Mark "McBeth" Bethell
315	David Richards
316	Barry Frenchman
317	David
318	Peter John Shirra
319	Robert Akers
320	Chris Clarke
321	Geoffrey Raynor
322	Robin, Jessica & Neil Harrison
323	Patrick (Paddy) Page
324	George Hurt
325	James Stevenson
326	Nigel Stott
327	Maurice Lindsay
328	Clive Nicholson
329	Derek Wallis
330	Stuart Astill
331	Leslie Webster
332	Alan Fisher
333	David Fletcher
334	Chris Spyron
335	Adrian Justin Killer
336	Paul Ancell
337	Mark Scrimshaw
338	Paul Tomlinson
339	John Hutchinson
340	Paul J Anderson
341	Stewart Holt - Newark on Trent
342	Patrick White
343	Alexander White
344	Andrew Weale
345	Krzysztof Pasternak
346	Riccardo Rossi
347	Angelo Stoitsis
348	Kevin Horton
349	Chris Wilson

350	Paul Robinson
351	Martin Preston
352	Pete Washington
353	Dave Taylor
354	David Nicholson
355	Ian Simpson
356	John Michael Hornbuckle
357	Steven Colin Hornbuckle
358	Michael Cobb
359	Val Eves
360	Mark A Hilton
361	Patrick Elliott
362	James Rushen
363	John Severn
364	Chris Ingle
365	Matthew Jackson
366	To Paul Underwood, Happy Christmas 2009, Love Anne, Lucy and Gemma
367	Curtis Scott Humphrey
368	Paul Stephen Gibson
369	Brian Tooby
370	George Harvey
371	Mike Forman
372	Liam Cox
373	Steve Prescott
374	Nottingham Central Library, local studies collection
375	Nottingham Central Library, local studies collection
376	Nottingham High School
377	Nottinghamshire Archive
378	Steve Hodge
379	Ian Preece
380	David Preece
381	Andy Johnson
382	Carl Froch

Thanks & Credits

As you'd probably expect with a book of this nature, there have been numerous people involved in all stages of the preparation of the finished article. Firstly we had many various institutions who allowed us the search through their collections and archives, some of which weren't necessarily football themed, but these often provided the rarest images and documents that we managed to unearth. The staff of these libraries and archives were generous with their time, helpful with their advice and patient enough to field our ever-more obscure questions and requests. We also received great help, and many rare images from the private collections of long-time fans and ex-players. The volume of material from these sources which was still growing as this project drew to a close ensured that we still have a wealth of unused material for future use. As usual we also received great help and advice from many sources at Nottingham Forest Football Club, including but not limited to proof-reading, advertising, permissions, sourcing of material and promotional assistance. The following list hopefully covers everyone who helped out as we already mentioned, and in other ways too: David Beaumont, Dave Brown, Tommy Capel, Gino Farabella, Nigel Fish, Mike Forman, Barry Frenchman, Mick Garton, Richard Harrison, Steve Hodge, Andy Johnson, Mick Jones, Carolyn Jovanovic, Billy Robertson, Ken Smales, Lucie Stones, Kezia Storr, Steve Tring, Mike West; the late Bob Fairhall, John Lawson, Fraser Nicholson, Geoff Peabody, Carolyn Peabody, Brandon Furse, Joe Sharphouse, Kevin Jackson and everyone at Nottingham Forest Football Club; Dorothy Ritchie and all the staff at the Nottingham Central Library; Yvette Gunther and the staff at the Nottingham High School; Mark Dorington and the staff of the Nottinghamshire Archive; Linda Shaw and the staff of the Manuscripts and Special Collections unit at the University of Nottingham; Martin Done, Matt Leadbeater, David Lowe, Carolyn Maginnis, Teresa Gorecka and everyone else at the Nottingham Evening Post; Nick Tomlinson and everyone at Picture the Past; Neil Walker and Angharad Jones at The University of Nottingham Collection; Paul White, Leon Gregory, Matt Tatler and all at Hickling & Squires. Many apologies to anyone we've missed out.

Picture Credits

Thanks are given to Topps and Panini for permission to use a selection of their cards and stickers. The school records and the Tinsley Lindley image on pages 8 and 28 are used by permision of Nottingham High School; the letter (Ga D 2482) reproduced on pages 14 and 15 is by permission of the Manuscripts and Special Collections unit at the University of Nottingham; the images used on pages 25 (CA/PL2) and 26 (CA/PL2) are by permission of the Nottinghamshire Archive; the images on pages 6-7, 9, 32-3, 50-1 and 88-9 are from Picture the Past and the ones on pages 11, 20, 21, 37, 70-1, 72, 75, 78 and 80-1 are used by permission of the Nottingham Central Library Local Studies Collection. The Forman brothers pictured on page 41 are by permission of Mike Forman. Other agency photos come from The Press Association, Action Images, JMS Photography and the Nottingham Evening Post. W.H.Revis by Marjorie Christine Bates (1883-1962) oil on canvas (page 12) by permission of The University of Nottingham Collection. All other images were provided by Nottingham Forest Football Club, the Pineapple Books Archive, Ken Smales, the Dave Beaumont Collection, the Richard Harrison collection and the Andy Johnson Collection.

www.picturethepast.org.uk

Index

Another Great Nottingham Team Making it Happen!

Hickling&Squires *print solutions*

Email hi@hickling-squires.co.uk
or call 01773 536400